Human Body

1000 FACTS

This edition published in 2008 by Miles Kelly Publishing Ltd
Bardfield Centre, Great Bardfield, Essex, CM7 4SL

Copyright © 2002 Miles Kelly Publishing Ltd

This material is also available in hardback

4 6 8 10 9 7 5 3

Editorial Director Belinda Gallagher
Art Director Jo Brewer
Volume Designer WhiteLight
Cover Designer Jo Brewer
Editorial Assistant Bethanie Bourne
Picture Researcher Liberty Newton
Reprographics Anthony Cambray, Mike Coupe,
Stephan Davis, Ian Paulyn
Production Manager Elizabeth Brunwin

British Library Cataloguing-in-Publication Data
A catalogue record for this book is available from the British Library

ISBN 978-1-84236-774-2

Printed in China

www.mileskelly.net
info@mileskelly.net

www.factsforprojects.com

Human Body

1000 FACTS

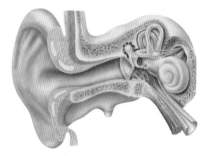

John Farndon

Consultant: Steve Parker

Miles Kelly
PUBLISHING

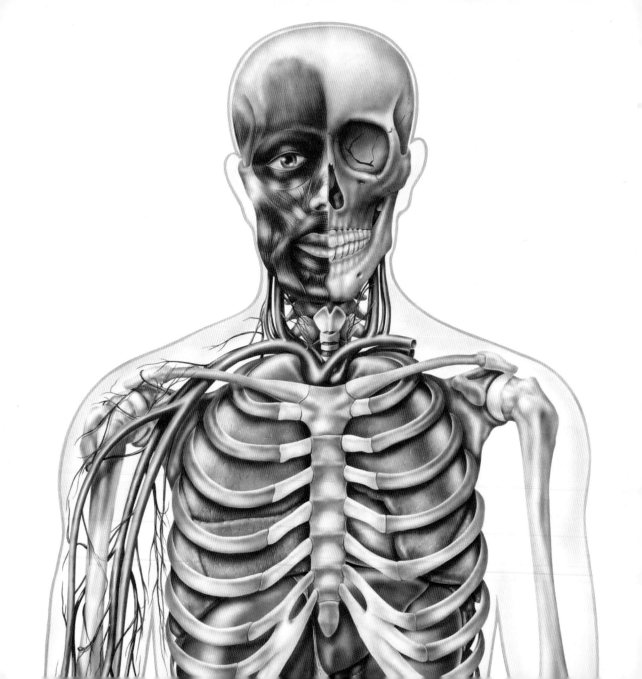

Contents

HEALTH AND DISEASE

BREATHING AND BLOOD

Contents

SKELETON AND MUSCLE

GROWING AND CHANGING

Body systems

▲ *Fresh air and exercise are vital for keeping our body systems working to their best potential.*

● **Your body systems** are interlinked – each has its own task, but they are all dependent on one another.

● **The skeleton** supports the body, protects the major organs, and provides an anchor for the muscles.

● **The nervous system** is the brain and the nerves – the body's control and communications network.

● **The digestive system** breaks down food into chemicals that the body can use to its advantage.

- **The immune system** is the body's defence against germs. It includes white blood cells, antibodies and the lymphatic system.

- **The urinary system** controls the body's water balance, removing extra water as urine and getting rid of impurities in the blood.

- **The respiratory system** takes air into the lungs to supply oxygen, and lets out waste carbon dioxide.

- **The reproductive system** is the smallest of all the systems. It is basically the sexual organs that enable people to have children. It is the only system that is different in men and women.

- **The other body systems** are the hormonal system (controls growth and internal co-ordination by chemical hormones), integumentary system (skin, hair and nails), and the sensory system (eyes, ears, nose, tongue, skin, balance).

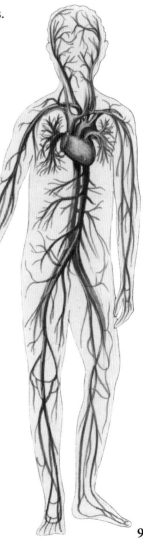

▶ *The cardiovascular system is the heart and the blood circulation. It keeps the body cells supplied with food and oxygen, and defends them against germs.*

...FASCINATING FACT...
The reproductive system is the only system that can be removed without threatening life.

Anatomy

- **Anatomy** is the study of the structure of the human body.

- **Comparative anatomy** compares the structure of our bodies to those of animals' bodies.

- **The first great anatomist** was the ancient Roman physician, Galen (AD 129–199).

- **The first great book** of anatomy was written in 1543 by the Flemish scientist Andreas Vesalius (1514–1564). It is called *De Humani Corporis Fabrica* ('On the Fabric of the Human Body.')

- **To describe the location** of body parts, anatomists divide the body into quarters.

- **The anatomical position** is the way the body is positioned to describe anatomical terms – upright, with the arms hanging down by the sides, and the eyes, palms and toes facing forwards.

Fig. 20

- **The central coronal plane** divides the body into front and back halves. Coronal planes are any slice across the body from side to side, parallel to the central coronal plane.

- **The ventral or anterior** is the front half of the body.

- **The dorsal or posterior** is the back half of the body.

- **Every part of the body** has a Latin name, but anatomists use a simple English name if there is one.

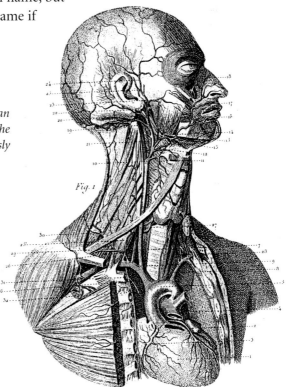

▶ *Much of our basic knowledge of human anatomy comes from the anatomists of the 16th and 17th centuries, who meticulously cut up corpses and then accurately drew what they saw.*

Fig. 1

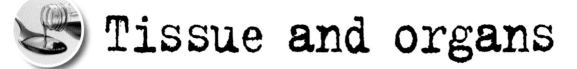

Tissue and organs

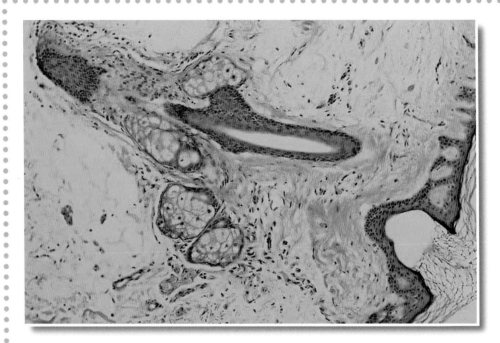

▲ *Skin, shown here in this highly-magnified photograph, is a complex form of ephithelial tissue.*

- **A tissue is a body substance** made from many of the same type of cell. Muscle cells make muscle tissue, nerve cells form nerve tissue, and so on.

- **As well as cells**, some tissues include other materials.

- **Connective tissues** are made from particular cells (such as fibroblasts), plus two other materials – long fibres of protein (such as collagen) and a matrix. Matrix is a material in which the cells and fibres are set like the currants in a bun.

▶ *Lungs are largely made from special lung tissues (see right), but the mucous membrane that lines the airways is epithelial tissue.*

- **Connective tissue** holds all the other kinds of tissue together in various ways. The adipose tissue that makes fat, tendons and cartilage is connective tissue.

- **Bone and blood** are both connective tissues.

- **Epithelial tissue** is good lining or covering material, making skin and other parts of the body.

- **Epithelial tissue** may combine three kinds of cell to make a thin waterproof layer – squamous (flat), cuboid (box-like) and columnar (pillar-like) cells.

- **Nerve tissue** is made mostly from neurons (nerve cells), plus the Schwann cells that coat them.

- **Organs** are made from combinations of tissues. The heart is made mostly of muscle tissue, but also includes epithelial and connective tissue.

...FASCINATING FACT...
All your body is made from tissue and tissue fluid (liquid that fills the space between cells).

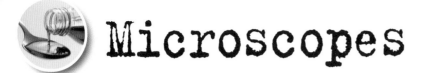

Microscopes

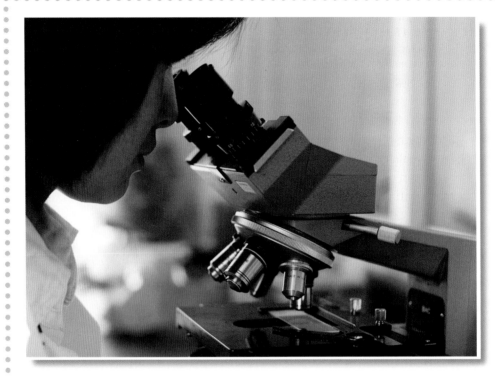

▲ *This optical microscope has several lenses so that it can give different magnifications. The lenses bend the light shining through the object before it reaches the eye.*

- **Optical microscopes** use lenses and light to magnify things (make them look bigger). By combining two or more lenses, they can magnify specimens up to 2000 times and reveal individual blood cells.

- **To magnify things more**, scientists use electron microscopes – microscopes that fire beams of tiny charged particles called electrons.

▶ *In this picture, a drop of blood has been placed between two glass slides. The slides will then be placed under an optical microscope to be viewed at a higher magnification.*

- **Electrons** have wavelengths 100,000 times smaller than light and so can give huge magnifications.

- **Scanning electron microscopes** (SEMs) are able to magnify things up to 100,000 times.

- **SEMs** show such things as the structures inside body cells.

- **Transmission electron microscopes** (TEMs) magnify even more than SEMs – up to 5 million times.

- **TEMs** can reveal the individual molecules in a cell.

- **SEM specimens** (things studied) must be coated in a special substance such as gold. They give a three-dimensional view.

- **Optical microscope specimens** are thinly sliced and placed between two glass slides. They give a cross-sectional view.

- **Microscopes help** to identify germs.

15

Cells

- **Cells** are the basic building blocks of your body. Most are so tiny you would need 10,000 to cover a pinhead.

- **There are over 200 different kinds** of cell in your body, including nerve cells, skin cells, blood cells, bone cells, fat cells, muscle cells and many more.

- **A cell is basically** a little parcel of organic (life) chemicals with a thin membrane (casing) of protein and fat. The membrane holds the cell together, but lets nutrients in and waste out.

- **Inside the cell** is a liquid called cytoplasm, and floating in this are various minute structures called organelles.

- **At the centre** of the cell is the nucleus – this is the cell's control centre and it contains the amazing molecule DNA (see genes). DNA not only has all the instructions the cell needs to function, but also has the pattern for new human life.

- **Each cell** is a dynamic chemical factory, and the cell's team of organelles is continually busy – ferrying chemicals to and fro, breaking up unwanted chemicals, and putting together new ones.

- **The biggest cells** in the body can be nerve cells. Although the main nucleus of nerve cells is microscopic, the tails of some cells can extend for a metre or more through the body, and be seen even without a microscope.

- **Among the smallest cells** in the body are red blood cells. These are just 0.0075 mm across and have no nucleus, since nearly their only task is ferrying oxygen.

- **Most body cells** live a very short time and are continually being replaced by new ones. The main exceptions are nerve cells – these are long-lived, but rarely replaced.

Mitochondria are the cell's power stations, turning chemical fuel supplied by the blood as glucose into energy packs of the chemical ATP (see muscle movement)

The endoplasmic reticulum is the cell's main chemical factory, where proteins are built under instruction from the nucleus

The ribosomes are the individual chemical assembly lines, where proteins are put together from basic chemicals called amino acids (see diet)

The nucleus is the cell's control centre, sending out instructions via a chemical called messenger RNA whenever a new chemical is needed

The lysosomes are the cell's dustbins, breaking up any unwanted material

The Golgi bodies are the cell's despatch centre, where chemicals are bagged up inside tiny membranes to send where they are needed

▲ *This illustration shows a typical cell, and some of the different organelles (special parts of a cell) that keep it working properly. The instructions come from the nucleus in the cell's control centre, but every kind of organelle has its own task.*

...FASCINATING FACT...
There are 75 trillion cells in your body!

Skin

▲ *Skin colour varies from person to person because of melanin, a pigment which protects skin from the sun's harmful rays. The more melanin you have in your skin, the darker it is.*

- **Skin is your protective coat,** shielding your body from the weather and from infection, and helping to keep it at just the right temperature.

- **Skin is your largest sense receptor**, responding to touch, pressure, heat and cold (see touch).

- **Skin makes** vitamin D for your body from sunlight.

- **The epidermis** (the thin outer layer) is just dead cells.

> ... **FASCINATING FACT** ...
> Even though its thickness averages just 2 mm, your skin gets an eighth of all your blood supply.

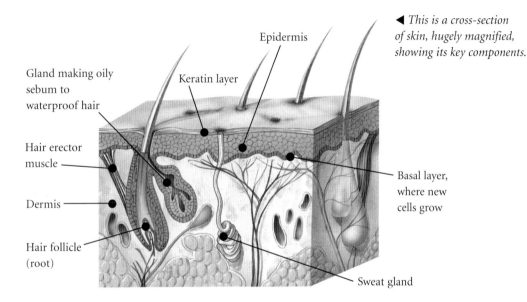

◄ *This is a cross-section of skin, hugely magnified, showing its key components.*

Epidermis

Gland making oily sebum to waterproof hair

Keratin layer

Hair erector muscle

Dermis

Hair follicle (root)

Basal layer, where new cells grow

Sweat gland

- **The epidermis is made mainly** of a tough protein called keratin – the remains of skin cells that die off.

- **Below the epidermis** is a thick layer of living cells called the dermis, which contains the sweat glands.

- **Hair roots** have tiny muscles that pull the hair upright when you are cold, giving you goose bumps.

- **Skin is 6 mm thick** on the soles of your feet, and just 0.5 mm thick on your eyelids.

- **The epidermis** contains cells that make the dark pigment melanin – this gives dark-skinned people their colour and fair-skinned people a tan.

19

Hair

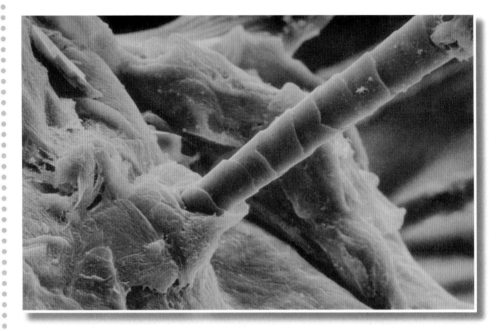

▲ *This highly magnified photograph shows a human hair growing from inside the skin.*

- **Humans are one of** very few land mammals to have almost bare skin. But even humans have soft, downy hair all over, with thicker hair in places.

- **Lanugo** is the very fine hair babies are covered in when they are inside the womb, from the fourth month of pregnancy onwards.

- **Vellus hair** is fine, downy hair that grows all over your body until you reach puberty.

- **Terminal hair** is the coarser hair on your head, as well as the hair that grows on men's chins and around an adult's genitals.

- **The colour of your hair** depends on how much there are of pigments called melanin and carotene in the hairs.

- **Hair is red or auburn** if it contains carotene.

- **Black, brown and blonde hair** get its colour from black melanin.

- **Each hair** is rooted in a pit called the hair follicle. The hair is held in place by its club-shaped tip, the bulb.

- **Hair grows** as cells fill with a material called keratin and die, and pile up inside the follicle.

- **The average person** has 120,000 head hairs and each grows about 3 millimetres per week.

▲ *The colour of your hair depends upon melanin made in melanocytes at the root.*

21

The skeleton

- **Your skeleton** is a rigid framework of bones, which provides an anchor for your muscles, supports your skin and other organs, and protects vital organs.

- **An adult's skeleton has 206 bones** joined together by rubbery cartilage. Some people have extra vertebrae (the bones of the backbone, or spine).

- **A baby's skeleton has 300** or more bones, but some of these fuse (join) together as the baby grows.

- **The parts of an adult skeleton** that have fused into one bone include the skull and the pelvis (see the skull). The pelvis came from fusing the ilium bones, the ischium bones and the pubis. The ischium is the bone that you sit on.

▶ *Your skeleton is the remarkably light, but very tough framework of bones that supports your body. It is made up of more than 200 bones.*

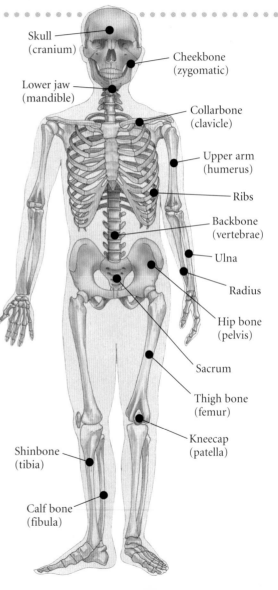

Skull (cranium)

Cheekbone (zygomatic)

Lower jaw (mandible)

Collarbone (clavicle)

Upper arm (humerus)

Ribs

Backbone (vertebrae)

Ulna

Radius

Hip bone (pelvis)

Sacrum

Thigh bone (femur)

Kneecap (patella)

Shinbone (tibia)

Calf bone (fibula)

- **The skeleton** has two main parts – the axial and the appendicular skeleton.

- **The axial skeleton** is the 80 bones of the upper body. It includes the skull, the vertebrae of the backbone, the ribs and the breastbone. The arm and shoulder bones are suspended from it.

- **The appendicular skeleton** is the other 126 bones – the arm and shoulder bones, and the leg and hip bones. It includes the femur (thigh bone), the body's longest bone.

- **The word skeleton** comes from the Ancient Greek word for 'dry'.

- **Most women and girls** have smaller and lighter skeletons than men and boys. But in women and girls, the pelvis is much wider than in men and boys. This is because the opening has to be wide enough for a baby to pass through when it is born.

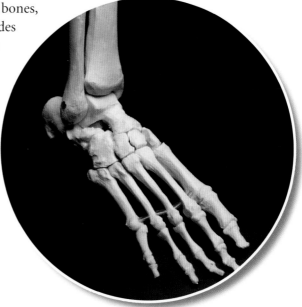

▲ *There are 14 bones in the toes, and 12 in the sole and the ankle, making 26 bones altogether that can be seen in this photograph.*

23

Bone

- **Bones are so strong** that they can cope with twice the squeezing pressure that granite can, or four times the stretching tension that concrete can.

- **Weight for weight,** bone is at least five times as strong as steel.

- **Bones are so light** they only make up 14% of your body's total weight.

- **Bones get their rigidity** from hard deposits of minerals such as calcium and phosphate.

▶ *Bones are strong but very light because, on the inside, they have many holes.*

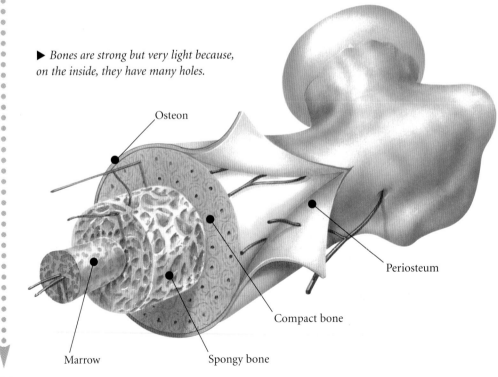

Osteon

Periosteum

Compact bone

Marrow

Spongy bone

- **Bones get their flexibility** from tough, elastic, rope-like fibres of collagen.

- **The hard outside of bones** (called compact bone) is reinforced by strong rods called osteons.

- **The inside of bones** (called spongy bone) is a light honeycomb, made of thin struts or trabeculae, perfectly angled to take stress.

- **The core of some bones,** such as the long bones in an arm or leg, is called bone marrow. It is soft and jelly-like.

- **In some parts of each bone,** there are special cells called osteoblasts which make new bone. In other parts, cells called osteoclasts break up old bone.

- **Bones grow** by getting longer near the end, at a region called the epiphyseal plate.

▲ *Milk contains a mineral called calcium, which is essential for building strong bones. Babies and children need plenty of calcium to help their bones develop properly.*

25

Marrow

- **Marrow** is the soft, jelly-like tissue in the middle of certain bones.

- **Bone marrow can be red** or yellow, depending on whether it has more blood tissue or fat tissue.

- **Red bone marrow** is the body's factory, where all blood cells apart from some white cells are made.

- **All bone marrow** is red when you are a baby, but as you grow older, more and more turns yellow.

- **In adults,** red marrow is only found in the ends of the limbs' long bones, breastbone, backbone, ribs, shoulder blades, pelvis and the skull.

- **Yellow bone marrow** is a store for fat, but it may turn to red marrow when you are ill.

- **All the different** kinds of blood cell start life in red marrow as one type of cell called a stem cell. Different blood cells then develop as the stem cells divide and re-divide.

- **Some stem cells** divide to form red blood cells and platelets.

- **Some stem cells** divide to form lymphoblasts. These divide in turn to form various different kinds of white cells, such as monocytes and lymphocytes.

- **The white cells** made in bone marrow play a key part in the body's immune system. This is why bone-marrow transplants can help people with illnesses that affect their immune system.

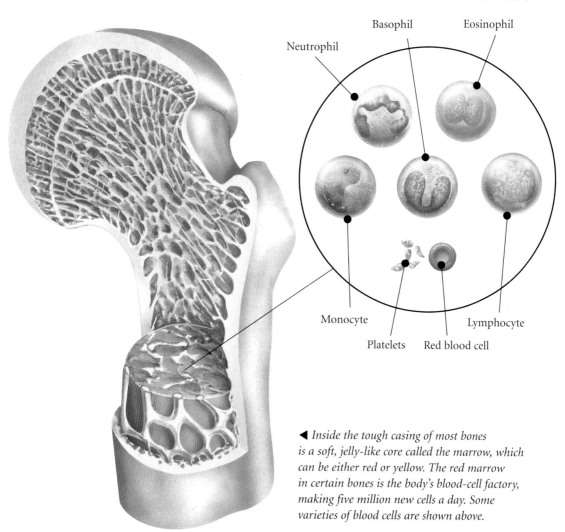

Neutrophil

Basophil

Eosinophil

Monocyte

Platelets

Red blood cell

Lymphocyte

◀ *Inside the tough casing of most bones is a soft, jelly-like core called the marrow, which can be either red or yellow. The red marrow in certain bones is the body's blood-cell factory, making five million new cells a day. Some varieties of blood cells are shown above.*

27

The skull

- **The skull** or cranium is the hard, bone case that contains and protects your brain.

- **The skull look**s as though it is a single bone. In fact, it is made up of 22 separate bones, cemented together along rigid joints called sutures.

- **The dome on top** is called the cranial vault and it is made from eight curved pieces of bone fused (joined) together.

- **As well as the sinuses** of the nose (see airways), the skull has four large cavities – the cranial cavity for the brain, the nasal cavity (the nose) and two orbits for the eyes.

- **There are holes in the skull** to allow blood vessels and nerves through, including the optic nerves to the eyes and the olfactory tracts to the nose.

> ...**FASCINATING FACT**...
> A baby has soft spots called fontanelles in its skull because the bones join slowly over about 18 months.

▲ *Skulls vary in size and shape. A bigger skull does not necessarily mean a person is more intelligent.*

- **The biggest hole** is in the base. It is called the foramen magnum, and the brain stem goes through it to meet the spinal cord.

- **In the 19th century**, people called phrenologists thought they could work out people's characters from little bumps on their skulls.

- **Archaeologists** can reconstruct faces from the past using computer analysis of ancient skulls.

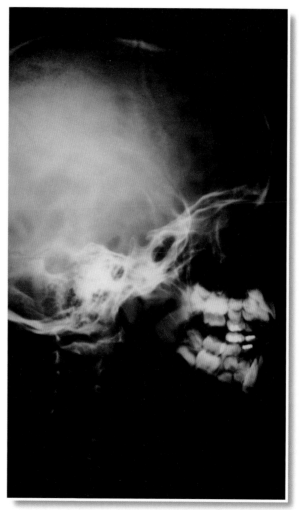

▶ *A child's skull, shown here in this X-ray photo, is quite large in relation to the rest of the child's body. As our bodies grow, our skull starts to look smaller in proportion.*

29

Backbone

- **The backbone**, otherwise known as the spine, extends from the base of the skull down to the hips.

- **The backbone is not a single bone,** but a column of drum-shaped bones called vertebrae (singular, vertebra).

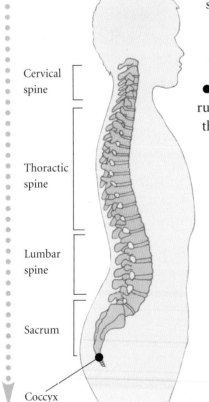

Cervical spine

Thoracic spine

Lumbar spine

Sacrum

Coccyx

- **There are 33 vertebrae** altogether, although some of these fuse or join as the body grows.

- **Each vertebra** is linked to the next by small facet joints, which are like tiny ball-and-socket joints.

- **The vertebrae are separated** by discs of rubbery material called cartilage. These cushion the bones when you run and jump.

- **The bones of the spine** are divided into five groups from top to bottom. These are the cervical (7 bones), the thoracic (12 bones), the lumbar (5 bones), the sacrum (5 bones fused together), and the coccyx (4 bones fused together).

- **The cervical spine** is the vertebrae of the neck. The thoracic spine is the back of the chest, and each bone has a pair of ribs attached to it. The lumbar spine is the small of the back.

◀ *The backbone is not straight – instead, its 33 vertebrae curve into an S-shape.*

● **A normal spine** curves in an
S-shape, with the cervical spine
curving forwards, the thoracic
section curving backwards, the
lumbar forwards, and the sacrum
curving backwards.

> **FASCINATING FACT**
> The story character the Hunchback of
> Notre Dame suffered from kyphosis –
> excessive curving of the spine.

● **On the back** of each vertebra is a bridge called the spinal process.
The bridges on each bone link together to form a tube which holds
the spinal cord, the body's central bundle of nerves.

▲ *Stretching keeps the joints in your back supple and helps to release tension.*

Ribs

- **The ribs** are the thin, flattish bones that curve around your chest.

- **Together,** the rib bones make up the rib cage.

- **The rib cage** protects the backbone and breastbone, as well as your vital organs – heart, lungs, liver, kidneys, stomach, spleen and so on.

- **You have 12 pairs** of ribs altogether.

- **Seven pairs** are called true ribs. Each rib is attached to the breastbone in front and curves around to join on to one of the vertebrae that make up the backbone via a strip of costal cartilage.

- **There are three pairs** of false ribs. These are attached to vertebrae but are not linked to the breastbone. Instead, each rib is attached to the rib above it by cartilage.

- **There are two pairs** of floating ribs. These are attached only to the vertebrae of the backbone.

- **The gaps between** the ribs are called intercostal spaces, and they contain thin sheets of muscle which expand and relax the chest during breathing.

- **Flail chest** is when many ribs are broken (often in a car accident) and the lungs heave the chest in and out.

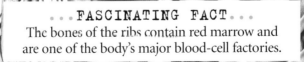

....FASCINATING FACT....
The bones of the ribs contain red marrow and
are one of the body's major blood-cell factories.

▶ *The ribs provide a framework for the chest and form a protective cage around the heart, lungs and other organs.*

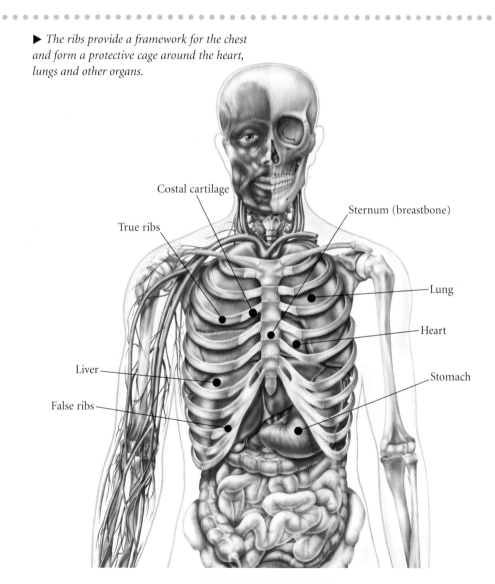

Costal cartilage

Sternum (breastbone)

True ribs

Lung

Heart

Liver

Stomach

False ribs

Joints

▶ *Gymnasts must have supple, flexible joints in order to achieve extreme positions like this.*

- **Body joints** are places where bones meet.
- **The skull** is not one bone, but 22 separate bones bound tightly together with fibres so that they cannot move.
- **Most body joints** (apart from fixed joints like the skull's fibrous joints) let bones move, but different kinds of joint let them move in different ways.
- **Hinge joints,** such as the elbow, let the bones swing to and fro in two directions like door hinges do.

- **In ball-and-socket joints,** such as the shoulder and hip, the rounded end of one bone sits in the cup-shaped socket of the other, and can move in almost any direction.

- **Swivel joints** turn like a wheel on an axle. Your head can swivel to the left or to the right on your spine.

- **Saddle joints** such as those in the thumb have the bones interlocking like two saddles. These joints allow great mobility with considerable strength.

- **The relatively inflexible joints** between the bones (vertebrae) of the spine are cushioned by pads of cartilage.

- **Synovial joints** are flexible joints such as the hip-joint, lubricated with oily 'synovial fluid' and cushioned by cartilage.

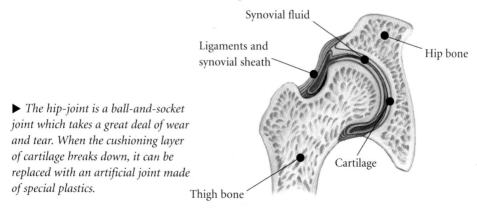

Synovial fluid

Ligaments and synovial sheath

Hip bone

Cartilage

Thigh bone

▶ *The hip-joint is a ball-and-socket joint which takes a great deal of wear and tear. When the cushioning layer of cartilage breaks down, it can be replaced with an artificial joint made of special plastics.*

Cartilage

- **Cartilage is a rubbery** substance used in various places around the body. You can feel cartilage in your ear if you move it back and forward.

- **Cartilage is made** from cells called chondrocytes embedded in a jelly-like ground substance with fibres of collagen, all wrapped in an envelope of tough fibres.

- **There are three types:** hyaline, fibrous and elastic.

- **Hyaline cartilage** is the most widespread in your body. It is almost clear, pearly white and quite stiff.

- **Hyaline cartilage** is used in many of the joints and ribs between bones to cushion them against impacts.

▼ *A single blow to the nose can easily damage the nasal cartilage, as often happens to boxers.*

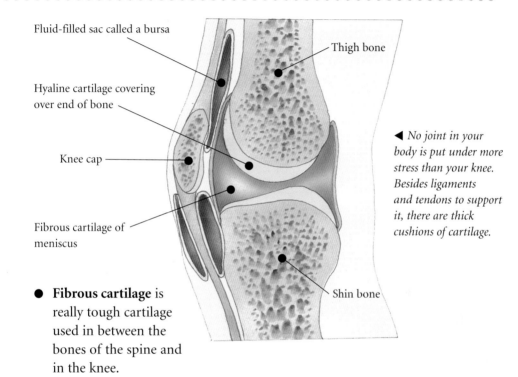

Fluid-filled sac called a bursa

Thigh bone

Hyaline cartilage covering over end of bone

◀ No joint in your body is put under more stress than your knee. Besides ligaments and tendons to support it, there are thick cushions of cartilage.

Knee cap

Fibrous cartilage of meniscus

Shin bone

- **Fibrous cartilage** is really tough cartilage used in between the bones of the spine and in the knee.

- **Cartilage in the knee** makes two dish shapes called a menisci between the thigh and shin bones. Footballers often damage these cartilages.

- **Elastic cartilage** is very flexible and used in your airways, nose and ears.

- **Cartilage grows** quicker than bone, and the skeletons of babies in the womb are mostly cartilage, which gradually ossifies (hardens to bone).

- **Osteoarthritis** is when joint cartilage breaks down, making certain movements painful.

Muscles

- **Muscles are special fibres** that contract (tighten) and relax to move parts of the body.

- **Voluntary muscles** are all the muscles you can control by will or thinking, such as your arm muscles.

- **Involuntary muscles** are the muscles you cannot control at will, but work automatically, such as the muscles that move food through your intestine.

- **Most voluntary muscles** cover the skeleton and are therefore called skeletal muscles. They are also called striated (striped) muscle because there are dark bands on the bundles of fibre that form them.

- **Most involuntary muscles** form sacs or tubes such as the intestine or the blood vessels. They are called smooth muscle because they lack the bands or stripes of voluntary muscles.

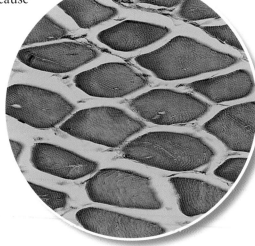

▶ *This microscopic cross-section shows striated, or striped, skeletal muscle. It is so-called because its fibres are made of light and dark stripes.*

38

- **Most muscles are arranged in pairs,** because although muscles can shorten themselves, they cannot forcibly make themselves longer. So the flexor muscle that bends a joint is paired with an extensor muscle to straighten it out again.

- **Heart muscle** is a unique combination of skeletal and smooth muscle. It has its own built-in contraction rhythm of 70 beats a minute, and special muscle cells that work like nerve cells for transmitting the signals for waves of muscle contraction to sweep through the heart.

  Your body's longest muscle is the sartorius on the inner thigh.

- **Your body's widest muscle** is the external oblique which runs around the side of the upper body.

- **Your body's biggest muscle** is the gluteus maximus in your buttock (bottom).

  ▶ *You have more than 640 skeletal muscles and they make up over 40% of your body's entire weight, covering your skeleton like a bulky blanket. The illustration here shows only the main surface muscles of the back, but your body has at least two layers, and sometimes three layers, of muscle beneath its surface muscles. Most muscles are firmly anchored at both ends and attached to the bones either side of a joint, either directly or via tough fibres called tendons.*

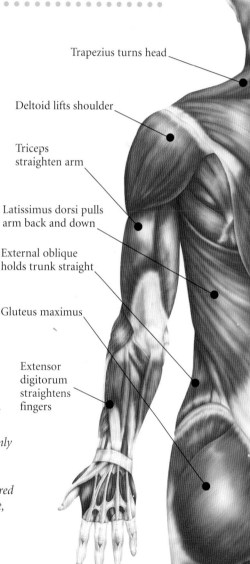

Trapezius turns head

Deltoid lifts shoulder

Triceps straighten arm

Latissimus dorsi pulls arm back and down

External oblique holds trunk straight

Gluteus maximus

Extensor digitorum straightens fingers

Muscle movement

▲ *Athletes sometimes suffer from muscle fatigue, when their muscles are overworked.*
This is caused by a build-up of lactic acid, a waste product made when muscles contract.

- **Most muscles are long and thin** and they work by pulling themselves shorter – sometimes contracting by up to half their length.

- **Skeletal muscles,** the muscles that make you move, are made of special cells which have not just one nucleus like other cells do, but many nuclei in a long fibre, called a myofibre.

- **Muscles are made** from hundreds or thousands of these fibres bound together like fibres in string.

- **Muscle fibres** are made from tiny strands called myofibrils, each marked with dark bands, giving the muscle its name of stripey or 'striated' muscle.

- **The stripes** in muscle are alternate bands of filaments of two substances: actin and myosin.

- **The actin and myosin** interlock, like teeth on a zip.

- **When a nerve signal** comes from the brain, chemical 'hooks' on the myosin twist and yank the actin filaments along, shortening the muscle.

- **The chemical hooks** on myosin are made from a stem called a cross-bridge and a head made of a chemical called adenosine triphosphate or ATP.

- **ATP is sensitive to calcium,** and the nerve signal from the brain that tells the muscle to contract does its work by releasing a flood of calcium to trigger the ATP.

> . . . **FASCINATING FACT** . . .
> If all the muscles in your body pulled together, they could lift a bus.

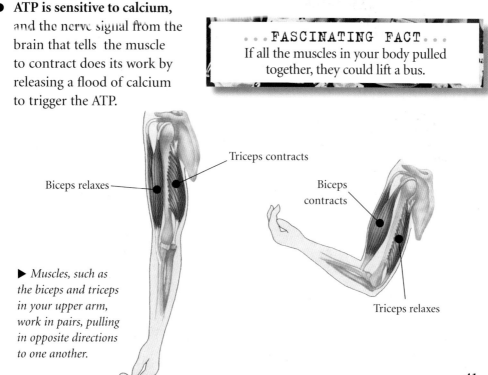

Biceps relaxes

Triceps contracts

Biceps contracts

Triceps relaxes

▶ *Muscles, such as the biceps and triceps in your upper arm, work in pairs, pulling in opposite directions to one another.*

41

The arm

- **The arm is made** from three long bones, linked by a hinge joint at the elbow.

- **The two bones** of the lower arm are the radius and the ulna.

- **The radius** supports the thumb side of the wrist.

- **The ulnar** supports the outside of the wrist.

- **The wrist** is one of the best places to test the pulse, since major arteries come nearer the surface here than at almost any other place in the body.

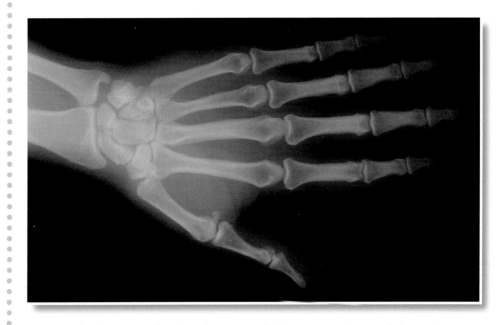

▲ *The intricate network of bones in your hands enables you to perform delicate and complex movements like writing or playing a musical instrument.*

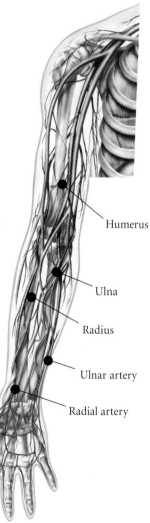

...FASCINATING FACT...
The upper arm bone is called the humerus
or, jokingly, the funny bone.

- **The two major muscles** of the upper arm are the
  biceps (which bends the elbow) and the triceps
  (which straightens it).

- **The hand is made** from 26 bones, including the
  carpals (wrist bones), the metacarpals (hand bones)
  and the phalanges (finger bones).

- **There are no strong muscles** in the hand. When you
  grip firmly, most of the power comes from muscles
  in the lower arm, linked to the bones of the hand
  by long tendons.

- **The shoulder** is one of the most flexible but least
  stable joints of the skeleton, since it is set in
  a very shallow socket. But it is supported by six
  major muscle groups, including the powerful
  deltoid (shoulder) muscle.

Humerus

Ulna

Radius

Ulnar artery

Radial artery

▶ *Look at the inside of your wrist on a warm day
and you may be able to see the radial artery
beneath the skin.*

43

Reflexes

▲ *Many sportsmen rely on lightning reflexes – actions too fast for the brain to even think about.*

- **Reflexes** are muscle movements that are automatic (they happen without you thinking about them).

- **Inborn reflexes** are reflexes you were born with, such as urinating or shivering when you are cold.

- **The knee-jerk** is an inborn reflex that makes your leg jerk up when the tendon below your knee is tapped.

- **Primitive reflexes** are reflexes that babies have for a few months after they are born.

- **One primitive reflex** is when you put something in a baby's hand and it automatically grips it.

- **Conditioned reflexes** are those you learn through habit, as certain pathways in the nervous system are used again and again.

- **Conditioned reflexes** help you do anything from holding a cup to playing football without thinking.

- **Reflex reactions** make you pull your hand from hot things before you have had time to think about it.

- **Reflex reactions** work by short-circuiting the brain. The alarm signal from your hand sets off motor signals in the spinal cord to move the hand.

- **A reflex arc** is the nerve circuit from sense to muscle via the spinal cord.

6. Brain is informed a split second later

4. Motor nerve

3. Reflex connection in spinal cord

5. Muscle pulls hand away

1. Pain sensor

2. Sensory nerve

▶ *If you touch a sharp pin, a message is fired along your sensory nerve to your spinal cord. A motor nerve then moves your hand away immediately. This response is a reflex action.*

45

Tendons and ligaments

- **Tendon**s are cords that tie a muscle to a bone or tie a muscle to another muscle.

- **Most tendons** are round, rope-like bundles of fibre. A few, such as the ones in the abdomen wall, are flat sheets called aponeuroses.

- **Tendon fibres are made** from a rubbery substance called collagen.

- **Your fingers are moved** mainly by muscles in the forearm, which are connected to the fingers by long tendons.

▲ *Tendons provide a link between muscle and bone. They prevent muscles tearing when they are put under strain.*

... FASCINATING FACT ...
The Achilles tendon is named after the Greek hero Achilles whose only weakness was his heel.

- **The Achilles tendon** pulls up your heel at the back.

- **Ligaments** are cords attached to bones on either side of a joint. They strengthen the joint.

- **Ligaments** also support various organs, including the liver, bladder and uterus (womb).

- **Women's breasts** are held in shape by bundles of ligaments.

- **Ligaments are made up** of bundles of tough collagen and a stretchy substance called elastin.

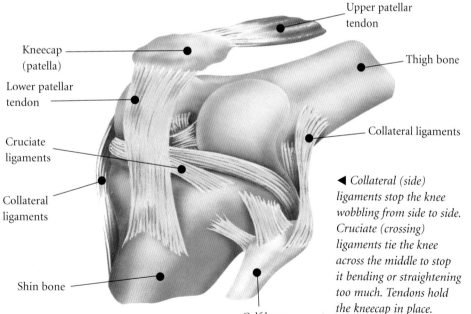

Upper patellar tendon

Kneecap (patella)

Thigh bone

Lower patellar tendon

Collateral ligaments

Cruciate ligaments

Collateral ligaments

◄ *Collateral (side) ligaments stop the knee wobbling from side to side. Cruciate (crossing) ligaments tie the knee across the middle to stop it bending or straightening too much. Tendons hold the kneecap in place.*

Shin bone

Calf bone

47

Breathing

- **You breathe** because every single cell in your body needs a continuous supply of oxygen to burn glucose, the high-energy substance from digested food that cells get from blood.

- **Scientists** call breathing 'respiration'. Cellular respiration is the way that cells use oxygen to burn glucose.

- **The oxygen in air** is taken into your lungs, and then carried in your blood to your body cells.

- **Waste carbon dioxide** from your cells is returned by your blood to your lungs, to be breathed out.

- **On average** you breathe in about 15 times a minute. If you run hard, the rate soars to around 80 times a minute.

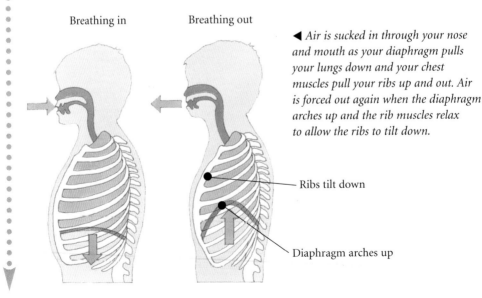

Breathing in　　　Breathing out

◀ *Air is sucked in through your nose and mouth as your diaphragm pulls your lungs down and your chest muscles pull your ribs up and out. Air is forced out again when the diaphragm arches up and the rib muscles relax to allow the ribs to tilt down.*

Ribs tilt down

Diaphragm arches up

- **Newborn babies** breathe about 40 times a minute.

- **If you live to the age of 80,** you will have taken well over 600 million breaths.

- **A normal breath** takes in about 0.4 litres of air. A deep breath can take in ten times as much.

- **Your diaphragm** is a dome-shaped sheet of muscle between your chest and stomach, which works with your chest muscles to make you breathe in and out.

- **Scientists** call breathing in 'inhalation', and breathing out 'exhalation'.

▶ *Wind musicians, such as this trumpeter, use their diaphragm and chest to control the air flowing in and out of their lungs. This allows them to produce a better quality sound.*

Airways

- **The upper airways** include the nose and the sinuses, the mouth and the pharynx (throat).

- **The lower airways** include the larynx (see vocal cords), the trachea (windpipe) and the airways of the lungs.

- **The sinuses** are air chambers within the bones of the skull that form the forehead and face.

...FASCINATING FACT...
Your throat is linked to your ears by tubes which open when you swallow to balance air pressure.

Thyroid bone

Muscles of larynx

Cartilages of larynx

Trachea

▶ *After air is taken in through the nose or mouth, it travels down the throat, down the windpipe held open by cartilage rings, and into the lungs.*

- **The soft palate** is a flap of tissue at the back of the mouth, which is pressed upwards when you swallow to stop food getting into your nose.

- **Your throat** is the tube that runs down through your neck from the back of your nose and mouth.

- **Your throat branches** in two at the bottom. One branch, the oesophagus, takes food to the stomach. The other, the larynx, takes air to the lungs.

- **The epiglottis** is the flap that tilts down to the larynx to stop food entering it when you swallow.

- **The tonsils and the adenoids** are bunches of lymph nodes (see lymphatic system) that swell to help fight ear, nose and throat infections, especially in young children.

- **The adenoids** are at the back of the nose, and the tonsils are at the back of the upper throat.

- **If tonsils or adenoids** swell too much, they are sometimes taken out.

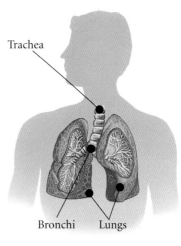

Trachea

Bronchi   Lungs

▲ *The lower airways include the larynx, the trachea (windpipe), and the bronchi which branch into the lungs.*

The vocal cords

- **Speaking and singing** depend on the larynx (voice-box) in your neck (see airways).

- **The larynx** has bands of stretchy fibrous tissue called the vocal cords, which vibrate (shake) as you breathe air out over them.

- **When you are silent**, the vocal cords are relaxed and apart, and air passes freely.

- **When you speak or sing,** the vocal cords tighten across the airway and vibrate to make sounds.

▶ *The vocal cords are soft flaps in the larynx, situated at the base of the throat. Our voices make sounds by vibrating these cords, as shown in the diagram.*

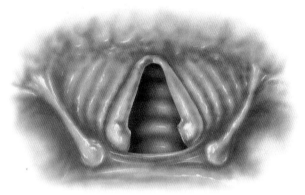

When the cords are apart no sound is made, as air can move freely past them

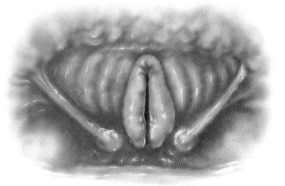

When the cords are pulled together by tiny muscles, air is forced through a small gap and the cords vibrate to create a sound

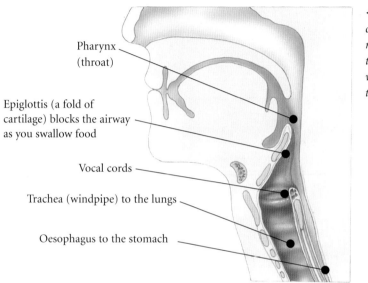

Pharynx (throat)

Epiglottis (a fold of cartilage) blocks the airway as you swallow food

Vocal cords

Trachea (windpipe) to the lungs

Oesophagus to the stomach

◀ *This shows a cross-section of your mouth, nose and throat, with the vocal cords at the top of the trachea.*

- **The tighter** the vocal cords are stretched, the less air can pass through them, so the higher pitched the sounds you make.

- **The basic sound** produced by the vocal cords is a simple 'aah'. But by changing the shape of your mouth, lips and especially your tongue, you can change this simple sound into letters and words.

- **Babies' vocal cords** are just 6 mm long.

- **Women's vocal cords** are about 20 mm long.

- **Men's vocal cords** are about 30 mm long. Because men's cords are longer than women's, they vibrate more slowly and give men deeper voices.

- **Boys' vocal cords** are the same length as girls' until they are teenagers – when they grow longer, making a boy's voice 'break' and get deeper.

53

The lungs

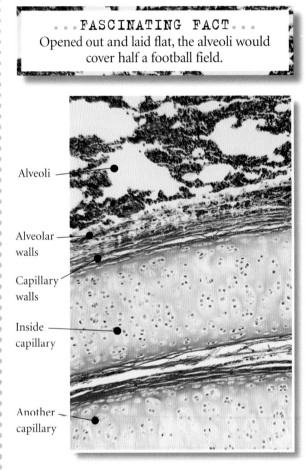

Alveoli

Alveolar
walls

Capillary
walls

Inside
capillary

Another
capillary

▲ *Taken through a powerful microscope, this
photo of a slice of lung tissue shows a blood vessel
and the very thin walls of an alveolus next to it.*

- **Your lungs** are a pair
  of soft, spongy bags
  inside your chest.

- **When you breathe** in,
  air rushes in through
  your nose or mouth,
  down your windpipe
  and into the millions
  of branching airways
  in your lungs.

- **The two biggest
  airways** are called
  bronchi (singular
  bronchus), and they
  both branch into
  smaller airways called
  bronchioles.

- **The surface of your
  airways** is protected by
  a slimy film of mucus,
  which gets thicker to
  protect the lungs when
  you have a cold.

- **At the end of each bronchiole** are bunches of minute air sacs called alveoli (singular alveolus).

- **Alveoli** are wrapped around with tiny blood vessels, and alveoli walls are just one cell thick – thin enough to let oxygen and carbon dioxide seep through them.

- **There are around 300 million alveoli** in your lungs.

- **The large surface area** of all these alveoli makes it possible for huge quantities of oxygen to seep through into the blood. Equally huge quantities of carbon dioxide can seep back into the airways for removal when you breathe out.

Windpipe

Lung

Main bronchus

Bronchial tubes

Diaphragm (main breathing muscle)

▶ *A front view of the lungs shows how they take up most of the room in the chest, being one of our most vital organs.*

55

Circulation

- **Your circulation** is the system of tubes called blood vessels which carries blood out from your heart to all your body cells and back again.

- **Blood circulation** was discovered in 1628 by the English physician William Harvey (1578–1657), who built on the ideas of Matteo Colombo.

- **Each of the body's** 600 billion cells gets fresh blood continuously, although the blood flow is pulsating.

- **On the way out** from the heart, blood is pumped through vessels called arteries and arterioles.

- **On the way back** to the heart, blood flows through venules and veins.

- **Blood flows** from the arterioles to the venules through the tiniest tubes called capillaries.

- **The blood circulation** has two parts – the pulmonary and the systemic.

- **The pulmonary circulation** is the short section that carries blood which is low in oxygen from the right side of the heart to the lungs for 'refuelling'. It then returns oxygen-rich blood to the left side of the heart.

- **The systemic circulation** carries oxygen-rich blood from the left side of the heart all around the body, and returns blood which is low in oxygen to the right side of the heart.

- **Inside the blood,** oxygen is carried by the haemoglobin in red blood cells (see blood cells).

56

The pulmonary circulation takes blood to and from the lungs

Radial artery

Iliac vein

Femoral artery

Peroneal artery

For each outward-going artery there is usually an equivalent returning vein

The brain receives more blood than any other part of the body

Blood leaves the left side of the heart through a giant artery called the aorta

Blood returns to the heart through main veins called the vena cavae

Saphenous vein

◄ *Blood circulates continuously round and round your body, through an intricate series of tubes called blood vessels. Bright red, oxygen-rich blood is pumped from the left side of the heart through vessels called arteries and arterioles. Purplish-blue, low-in-oxygen blood returns to the right of the heart through veins and venules.*

▲ *Red blood cells can actually be brown in colour, but they turn bright scarlet when their haemoglobin is carrying oxygen. After the haemoglobin passes its oxygen to a cell, it fades to dull purple. So oxygen-rich blood from the heart is red, while oxygen-poor blood that is returning to the heart is a purplish-blue colour.*

Arteries

▶ *This illustration shows how the main kinds of blood vessel in the body are connected. The artery (red) branches into tiny capillaries, which join up to supply the vein (blue).*

Vein

Capillaries

Arteriole

Venule

Space within for blood

Endothelium (inner lining)

Artery

Thick muscle layer

Outer sheath

- **An artery** is a tube-like blood vessel that carries blood away from the heart.

- **Systemic arteries deliver oxygenated blood** around the body. Pulmonary arteries deliver deoxygenated blood to the lungs.

- **An arteriole** is a smaller branch off an artery. Arterioles branch into microscopic capillaries.

- **Blood flows through** arteries at 30 cm per second in the main artery, down to 2 cm or less per second in the arterioles.

- **Arteries run alongside** most of the veins that return blood to the heart.

- **The walls of arteries** are muscular and can expand or relax to control the blood flow.

- **Arteries have** thicker, stronger walls than veins, and the pressure of the blood in them is a lot higher.

- **Over-thickening of the artery walls** may be one of the causes of hypertension (high blood pressure).

- **In old age** the artery walls can become very stiff. This hardening of the arteries, called arteriosclerosis, can cut blood flow to the brain.

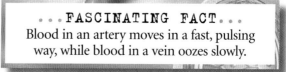

...FASCINATING FACT...
Blood in an artery moves in a fast, pulsing
way, while blood in a vein oozes slowly.

Capillaries

- **Capillaries** are the smallest of all your blood vessels, only visible under a microscope. They link the arterioles to the venules (see circulation).

- **Capillaries** were discovered by Marcello Malphigi in 1661.

- **There are 10 billion capillaries** in your body.

- **The largest capillary** is just 0.2 mm wide – thinner than a hair.

- **Each capillary** is about 0.5 mm to 1 mm long.

- **Capillary walls** are just one cell thick, so it is easy for chemicals to pass through them.

▲ *The work done by an athlete's muscles generates a lot of heat – which the body tries to lose by opening up capillaries in the skin, turning the skin bright red.*

. . . . FASCINATING FACT . . . .
The average capillary is 0.001 mm in diameter – just wide enough for red blood cells to pass through one at a time.

- **It is through the capillary walls** that your blood passes oxygen, food and waste to and from each one of your body cells.

- **There are many more capillaries** in active tissues such as muscles, liver and kidneys than there are in tendons and ligaments.

- **Capillaries** carry less or more blood according to need. They carry more to let more blood reach the surface when you are warm. They carry less to keep blood away from the surface and save heat when you are cold.

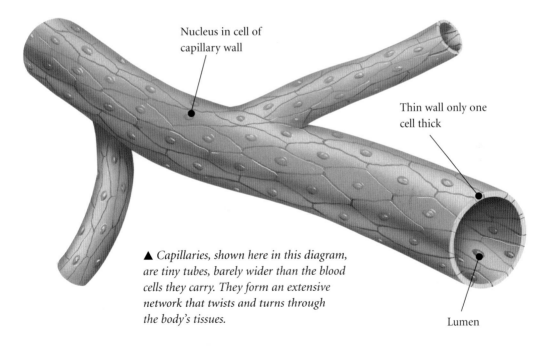

Nucleus in cell of capillary wall

Thin wall only one cell thick

▲ *Capillaries, shown here in this diagram, are tiny tubes, barely wider than the blood cells they carry. They form an extensive network that twists and turns through the body's tissues.*

Lumen

Veins

> ...FASCINATING FACT...
> At any moment, 75% of the body's blood is in the veins.

- **Veins** are pipes in the body for carrying blood back to the heart.

- **Unlike arteries,** most veins carry 'used' blood back to the heart – the body cells have taken the oxygen they need from the blood, so it is low in oxygen.

- **When blood** is low in oxygen, it is a dark, purplish blue colour – unlike the bright red of the oxygenated blood carried by the arteries.

- **The only veins** that carry oxygenated blood are the four pulmonary veins, which carry blood from the lungs the short distance to the heart.

- **The two largest veins** in the body are the vena cavae that flow into the heart from above and below.

▶ *This shows a greatly enlarged cutaway of a small vein. The valve prevents the blood from flowing backwards away from the heart.*

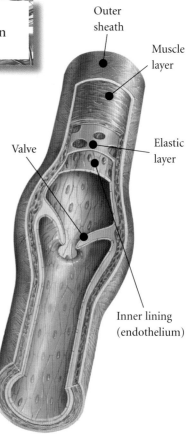

Outer sheath

Muscle layer

Valve

Elastic layer

Inner lining (endothelium)

- **Inside most veins** are flaps that act as valves to make sure that the blood only flows one way.

- **The blood in veins** is pumped by the heart, but the blood pressure is much lower than in arteries and vein walls do not need to be as strong.

- **Unlike arteries,** veins collapse when empty.

- **Blood is helped through** the veins by pressure that is placed on the vein walls by the surrounding muscles.

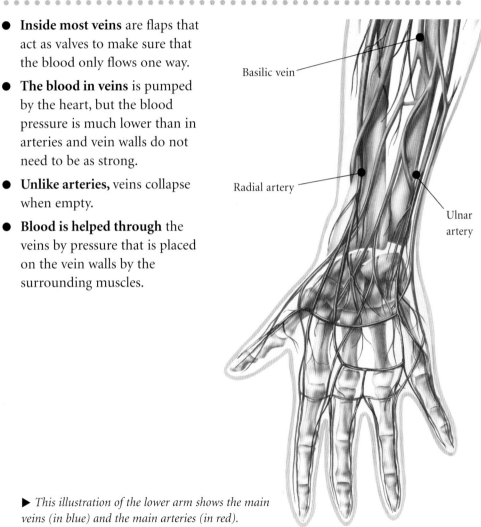

Basilic vein

Radial artery

Ulnar artery

▶ *This illustration of the lower arm shows the main veins (in blue) and the main arteries (in red).*

63

The heart

- **Your heart** is the size of your fist. It is inside the middle of your chest, slightly to the left.

- **The heart is a powerful pump** made almost entirely of muscle.

- **The heart contracts** (tightens) and relaxes automatically about 70 times a minute to pump blood out through your arteries.

- **The heart has two sides** separated by a muscle wall called the septum.

- **The right side** is smaller and weaker, and it pumps blood only to the lungs.

- **The stronger left side** pumps blood around the body.

- **Each side of the heart** has two chambers. There is an atrium (plural atria) at the top where blood accumulates (builds up) from the veins, and a ventricle below which contracts to pump blood out into the arteries.

- **Each side of the heart** (left and right) ejects about 70 ml of blood every beat.

- **There are two valves** in each side of the heart to make sure that blood flows only one way – a large one between the atrium and the ventricle, and a small one at the exit from the ventricle into the artery.

- **The coronary arteries** supply the heart. If they become clogged, the heart muscle may be short of blood and stop working. This is what happens in a heart attack.

> ...FASCINATING FACT...
> During an average lifetime, the heart pumps
> 200 million litres of blood – enough to fill
> New York's Central Park to a depth of 15 m.

Pulmonary artery takes blood to the lungs to pick up oxygen

Two big veins called the venae cavae bring blood low in oxygen back from the body to the right side of the heart

A large artery called the aorta sends blood rich in oxygen out to the whole body

Pulmonary veins bring blood back from the lungs

Blood loaded with oxygen from the lungs enters the left atrium

Tricuspid valve between the atrium and ventricle of the right side of the heart

Blood rich in oxygen returns from the lungs

Mitral valve between the atrium and ventricle of the left side of the heart

Right ventricle pumps blood to the lungs

Septum

Left ventricle pumps blood out to the whole body via the aorta

▲ The heart is a remarkable double pump, with two pumping chambers, the left and the right ventricles. It contracts automatically to squeeze jets of blood out of the ventricles and through the arteries.

65

Heartbeat

- **The heartbeat** is the regular squeezing of the heart muscle to pump blood around the body.

- **Four heart valves** make sure blood only moves one way.

- **The heartbeat** is a sequence called the cardiac cycle and it has two phases – systole and diastole.

- **Systole** is when the heart muscle contracts (tightens). Diastole is the resting phase between contractions.

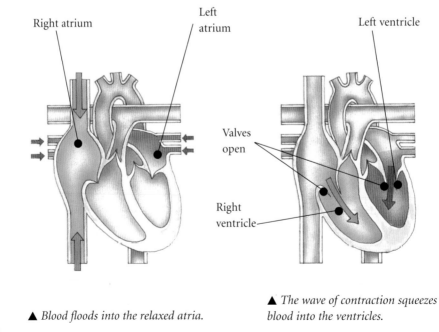

Right atrium

Left atrium

Left ventricle

Valves open

Right ventricle

▲ *Blood floods into the relaxed atria.*

▲ *The wave of contraction squeezes blood into the ventricles.*

- **Systole begins** when a wave of muscle contraction sweeps across the heart and squeezes blood from each of the atria into the two ventricles.

- **When the contraction** reaches the ventricles, they squeeze blood out into the arteries.

- **In diastole,** the heart muscle relaxes and the atria fill with blood again.

- **Heart muscle** on its own would contract automatically.

- **Nerve signals** make the heart beat faster or slower.

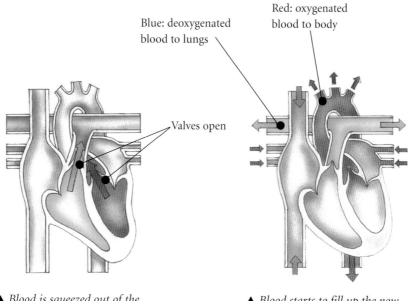

Blue: deoxygenated blood to lungs

Red: oxygenated blood to body

Valves open

▲ *Blood is squeezed out of the ventricles into the arteries.*

▲ *Blood starts to fill up the now relaxed atria again.*

Pulse

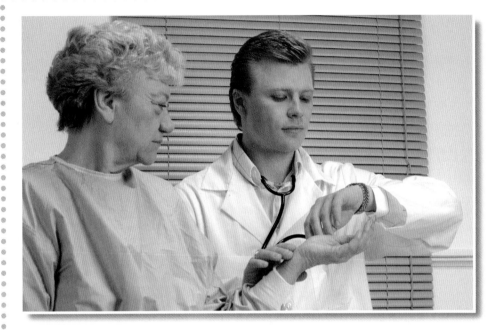

▲ *A doctor tests his patient's pulse rate by timing how many beats there are per minute.*

- **Your pulse** is the powerful high-pressure surge or wave that runs through your blood and vessels as the heart contracts strongly with each beat.

- **You can feel your pulse** by pressing two fingertips on the inside of your wrist where the radial artery nears the surface (see the arm).

- **Other pulse points** include the carotid artery in the neck and the brachial artery inside the elbow.

- **Checking the pulse** is a good way of finding out how healthy someone is, which is why doctors do it.

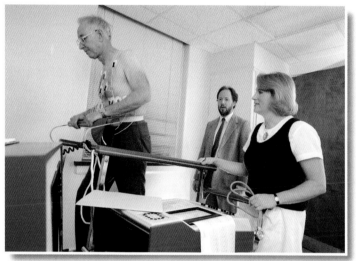

▶ *An ECG can show how healthy someone's heart is, by monitoring how much the heart rate goes up and down during exercise.*

- **Normal pulse rates** vary between 50 and 100 beats a minute. The average for a man is about 71, for a woman it is 80, and for children it is about 85.

- **Tachycardia** is the medical word for an abnormally fast heartbeat.

- **Someone who has tachycardia** when sitting down may have drunk too much coffee or tea, or taken drugs, or be suffering from anxiety or a fever, or have heart disease.

- **Bradycardia** is an abnormally slow heartbeat rate.

- **Arrhythmia** is any abnormality in a person's heartbeat rate.

- **Anyone with a heart problem** may be connected to a machine called an electrocardiogram (ECG) to monitor (watch) their heartbeat.

69

Blood

- **Blood** is the reddish liquid that circulates around your body. It carries oxygen and food to body cells, and takes carbon dioxide and other waste away. It fights infection, keeps you warm, and distributes chemicals that control body processes.

- **Blood is made up of** red cells, white cells and platelets, all carried in a liquid called plasma.

- **Plasma** is 90% water, plus hundreds of other substances, including nutrients, hormones and special proteins for fighting infection.

- **Blood plasma** turns milky immediately after a meal high in fats.

- **Platelets** are tiny pieces of cell that make blood clots start to form in order to stop bleeding.

◀ *A centrifuge is used to separate the different components of blood. The spinning action of the machine separates the heavier blood cells from the lighter plasma.*

● **Blood clots also** involve a lacy, fibrous network made from a protein called fibrin. Fibrin is set in action by a sequence of chemicals called factors (factors 1 through to 8).

● **The amount of blood** in your body depends on your size. An adult who weighs 80 kg has about 5 litres of blood. A child who is half as heavy has half as much blood.

▶ *Blood may look like a simple sticky red liquid, but it is actually a watery liquid containing millions of cells.*

● **A drop of blood** the size of the dot on this i contains around 5 million red cells.

● **If a blood donor** gives 0.5 litres of blood, the body replaces the plasma in a few hours, but it takes a few weeks to replace the red cells.

71

Blood cells

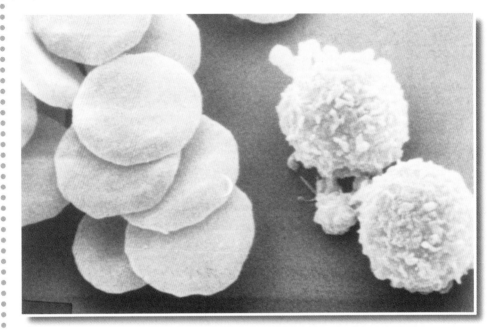

▲ *This is a highly magnified photograph of red blood cells (left) and white blood cells.*

- **Your blood has two main kinds of cell** – red cells and white cells – plus pieces of cell called platelets (see blood).

- **Red cells** are button-shaped and they contain mainly a red protein called haemoglobin.

- **Haemoglobin** is what allows red blood cells to ferry oxygen around your body.

- **Red cells** also contain enzymes which the body uses to make certain chemical processes happen (see enzymes).

- **White blood cells** are big cells called leucocytes and most types are involved in fighting infections.

- **Most white cells** contain tiny little grains and are called granulocytes.

- **Most granulocytes** are giant white cells called neutrophils. They are the blood's cleaners, and their task is to eat up invaders.

- **Eosinophils and basophils** are granulocytes that are involved in fighting disease. Some release antibodies that help fight infection (see antibodies).

- **Lymphocytes** are also types of white cells (see lymphocytes and antibodies).

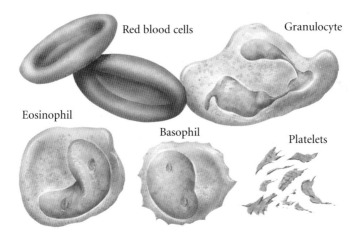

Red blood cells

Granulocyte

Eosinophil

Basophil

Platelets

▲ *These are some important kinds of cell in the blood – red cells, three kinds of white cells, and platelets.*

...FASCINATING FACT...
Each red blood cell contains more than 200 million molecules of haemoglobin.

Blood groups

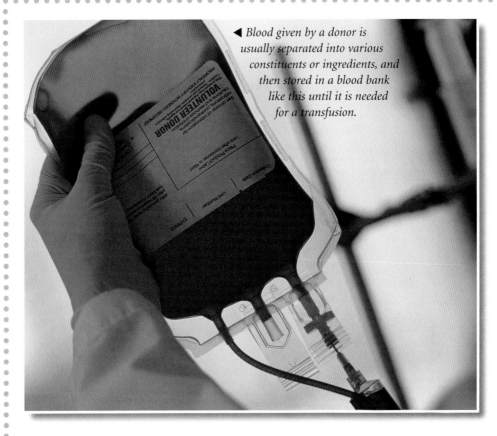

◀ *Blood given by a donor is usually separated into various constituents or ingredients, and then stored in a blood bank like this until it is needed for a transfusion.*

- **Most people's blood** belongs to one of four different groups or types – A, O, B and AB.

- **Blood type O** is the most common, followed by blood group A.

- **Blood is also** either Rhesus positive (Rh+) or Rhesus negative (Rh-).

- **Around 85% of people** are Rh+. The remaining 15% are Rh-.

- **If your blood is Rh+** and your group is A, your blood group is said to be A positive. If your blood is Rh- and your group is O, you are O negative, and so on.

- **The Rhesus factors** got their name because they were first identified in Rhesus monkeys.

- **A transfusion** is when you are given blood from another person's body. Your blood is 'matched' with other blood considered safe for transfusion.

- **Blood transfusions** are given when someone has lost too much blood due to an injury or operation. They are also given to replace diseased blood.

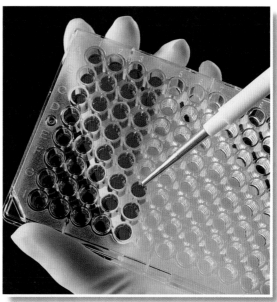

▶ *Donated blood is tested to determine its blood group. The blood must belong to a suitable group, otherwise patients undergoing a blood transfusion could become very ill.*

The lymphatic system

- **The lymphatic system** is your body's sewer, the network of pipes that drains waste from the cells.

- **The 'pipes' of the lymphatic system** are called lymphatics or lymph vessels.

- **The lymphatics** are filled by a watery liquid called lymph fluid which, along with bacteria and waste chemicals, drains from body tissues such as muscles.

- **The lymphatic system** has no pump, such as the heart, to make it circulate. Instead, lymphatic fluid is circulated as a side effect of the heartbeat and muscle movement.

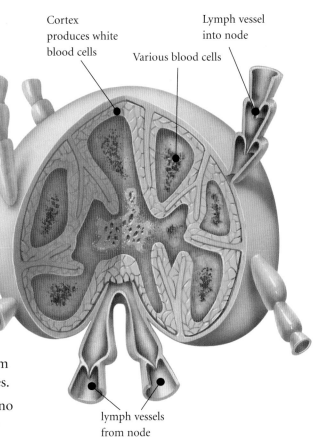

Cortex produces white blood cells

Various blood cells

Lymph vessel into node

lymph vessels from node

▲ *This shows a cross-section of a lymph node. White blood cells are produced and stored here, and are released through the lymph vessels into the bloodstream.*

- **At places** in the lymphatic system there are tiny lumps called nodes. These are filters which trap germs that have got into the lymph fluid.

- **In the nodes**, armies of white blood cells called lymphocytes neutralize or destroy germs.

- **When you have** a cold or any other infection, the lymph nodes in your neck or groin, or under your arm, may swell, as lymphocytes fight germs. This is sometimes called 'swollen glands'.

- **Lymph fluid** drains back into the blood via the body's main vein, the superior vena cava (see heart).

- **The lymphatic system** is not only the lymphatics and lymph nodes, but includes the spleen, the thymus, the tonsils and the adenoids (see the immune system).

- **On average**, at any time about 1 to 2 litres of lymph fluid circulate in the lymphatics and body tissues.

Drainage back into the blood system

Lymphatics (lymph vessels)

Concentrations of lymph nodes

Lymphatics (lymph vessels)

▶ *The lymphatic system is a branching network of little tubes that reaches throughout the body. It drains back to the centre of the body, running into the branches of the superior vena cava, the body's main vein to the heart.*

Digestion

- **Digestion** is the process by which your body breaks down the food you eat into substances that it can absorb (take in) and use.

- **Your digestive tract** is basically a long, winding tube called the alimentary canal (gut). It starts at your mouth and ends at your anus.

- **If you could lay** your gut out straight, it would be nearly six times as long as you are tall.

- **The food you eat** is softened in your mouth by chewing and by chemicals in your saliva (spit).

- **When you swallow,** food travels down your oesophagus (gullet) into your stomach. Your stomach is a muscular-walled bag which mashes the food into a pulp, helped by chemicals called gastric juices.

- **When empty,** your stomach holds barely 0.5 litres, but after a big meal it can stretch to more than 4 litres.

- **The half-digested food** that leaves your stomach is called chyme. It passes into your small intestine.

- **Your small intestine** is a 6-m-long tube where chyme is broken down into molecules small enough to be absorbed through the intestine wall into the blood.

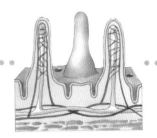

▲ *The small intestine is lined with tiny, finger-like folds called villi. On the surface of each villus are even tinier, finger-like folds called microvilli. These folds give a huge area for absorbing food.*

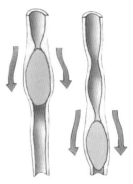

▲ *Food is pushed through the long, winding digestive tract by waves of contraction (tightening) that pass along its muscular walls. These waves are called peristalsis.*

... FASCINATING FACT ...
On average, food takes 24 hours to pass right the way through your alimentary canal and out the other end.

- **Food that cannot be** digested in your small intestine passes on into your large intestine. It is then pushed out through your anus as faeces when you go to the toilet (see excretion).

- **Digestive enzymes** play a vital part in breaking food down so it can be absorbed by the body.

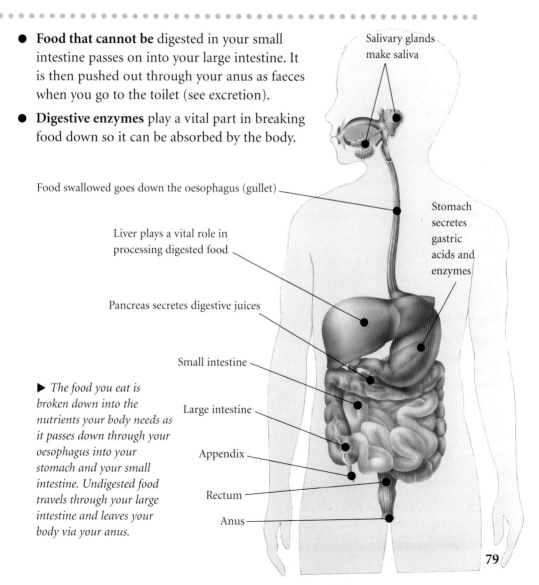

Salivary glands make saliva

Food swallowed goes down the oesophagus (gullet)

Stomach secretes gastric acids and enzymes

Liver plays a vital role in processing digested food

Pancreas secretes digestive juices

Small intestine

▶ *The food you eat is broken down into the nutrients your body needs as it passes down through your oesophagus into your stomach and your small intestine. Undigested food travels through your large intestine and leaves your body via your anus.*

Large intestine

Appendix

Rectum

Anus

79

Teeth

▶ *This shows one side of an adult's lower jaw. Not every adult grows the full set of eight teeth on each side of the jaw.*

First premolar

Second premolar

First and second molars

Third molar (wisdom tooth)

First incisor

Second incisor

Canine

- **Milk teeth** are the 20 teeth that start to appear when a baby is about six months old.

- **When you are six,** you start to grow your 32 adult teeth – 16 top in the top row and 16 in the bottom.

- **Molars** are the (usually) six pairs of big, strong teeth at the back of your mouth. Their flattish tops are a good shape for grinding food.

- **The four rearmost molars,** one in each back corner of each jaw, are the wisdom teeth. These are the last to grow and sometimes they never appear.

- **Premolars** are four pairs of teeth in front of the molars.

- **Incisors** are the four pairs of teeth at the front of your mouth. They have sharp edges for cutting food.

- **Canines** are the two pairs of big, pointed teeth behind the incisors. Their shape is good for tearing food.

- **The enamel** on teeth is the body's hardest substance.
- **Dentine** inside teeth is softer but still hard as bone.
- **Teeth** sit in sockets in the jawbones.

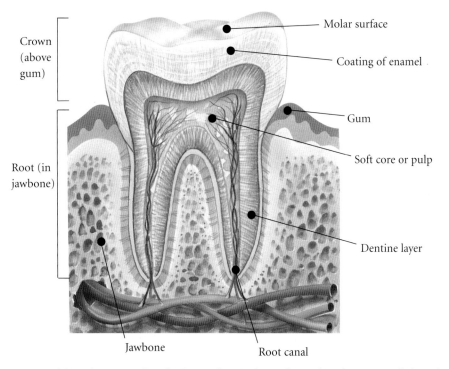

Crown
(above
gum)

Root (in
jawbone)

Molar surface

Coating of enamel

Gum

Soft core or pulp

Dentine layer

Jawbone

Root canal

▲ *Teeth have long roots that slot into sockets in the jawbones, but they sit in a fleshy ridge called the gums. In the centre of each tooth is a living pulp of blood and nerves. Around this is a layer of dentine, then on top of that a tough shield of enamel.*

The liver

▶ *The liver is a large organ situated to the right of the stomach.*

Right lobe

Left lobe

Dividing ligament

Bile duct

Gall bladder

Hepatic portal vein
(carries food-rich blood
from small intestine)

Hepatic artery
(brings oxygen-
rich blood from
the heart)

- **The liver** is your chemical processing centre.

- **The liver is your body's biggest internal organ,** and the word hepatic means 'to do with the liver'.

- **The liver's prime task** is handling all the nutrients and substances digested from the food you eat and sending them out to your body cells when needed.

- **The liver turns** carbohydrates into glucose, the main energy-giving chemical for body cells.

- **The liver keeps** the levels of glucose in the blood steady. It does this by releasing more when levels drop, and by storing it as glycogen, a type of starch, when levels rise.

- **The liver packs off** excess food energy to be stored as fat around the body.

- **The liver breaks down** proteins and stores vitamins and minerals.

▲ *The liver filters harmful substances such as alcohol and food additives to keep the body safe.*

- **The liver produces bile,** the yellowish or greenish bitter liquid that helps dissolve fat as food is digested in the intestines.

- **The liver clears the blood** of old red cells and harmful substances such as alcohol, and makes new plasma (see blood).

- **The liver's chemical processing units**, called lobules, take in unprocessed blood on the outside and dispatch it through a collecting vein.

The pancreas

- **The pancreas** is a large, carrot-shaped gland which lies just below your stomach.

- **The pancreas** is made from a substance called exocrine tissue, embedded with hundreds of nests of hormone glands called the islets of Langerhans.

- **The exocrine tissue** secretes (releases) pancreatic enzymes such as amylase into the intestine to help digest food (see enzymes).

- **Amylase** breaks down carbohydrates into simple sugars such as maltose, lactose and sucrose.

- **The pancreatic enzymes** run into the intestine via a pipe called the pancreatic duct, which joins on to the bile duct. This duct also carries bile (see liver).

- **The pancreatic enzymes** only start working when they meet other kinds of enzyme in the intestine.

▲ *This is a microscopic view of the pancreas, with the islets of Langerhans (shown in purple) embedded in the exocrine tissue.*

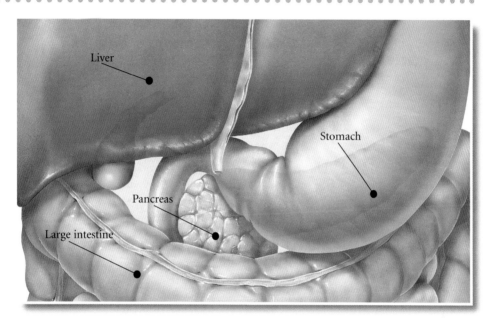

Liver

Stomach

Pancreas

Large intestine

▲ *The larger end of the pancreas is on the right-hand side of your body, tucking into the gut. The tail end is on the left, touching the spleen.*

● **The pancreas** also secretes the body's own antacid, sodium bicarbonate, to settle an upset stomach.

● **The islets of Langerhans** secrete two important hormones: insulin and glucagon.

● **Insulin and glucagon** regulate blood sugar levels (see glucose).

● **Diabetics** suffer from the condition diabetes. They produce little or no insulin in their pancreas but control their blood glucose by injecting insulin.

Diet

- **Your diet** is what you eat. A good diet includes the correct amount of proteins, carbohydrates, fats, vitamins, minerals, fibre and water.

- **Most of the food** you eat is fuel for the body, provided mostly by carbohydrates and fats.

- **Carbohydrates** are foods made from kinds of sugar, such as glucose and starch. They are found in foods such as bread, rice, potatoes and sweet things.

- **Fats** are greasy foods that will not dissolve in water. Some, such as the fats in meat and cheese, are solid. Some, such as cooking oil, are liquid.

- **Fats are not** usually burned up straight away, but are stored around your body until they are needed.

▲ *Carbohydrates (top), proteins (centre) and fats (left) are just some of the important food groups we need for a healthy diet.*

● **Proteins** are needed to build and repair cells. They are made from special chemicals called amino acids.

● **There are 20** different amino acids. Your body can make 11 of them. The other nine are called essential acids and they come from food.

● **Meat and fish** are very high in protein.

● **A correctly balanced vegetarian diet** of eggs, milk and cheese can provide all the essential amino acids.

● **Fibre or roughage** is supplied by cellulose from plant cell walls. Your body cannot digest fibre, but needs it to keep the bowel muscles exercised.

▲ *Fresh fruit and vegetables provide us with an assortment of vital vitamins and minerals.*

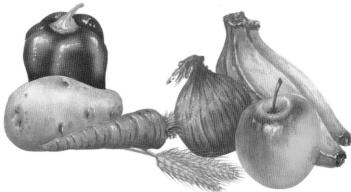

▶ *These foods contain fibre, which helps keep the digestive system healthy.*

Glucose

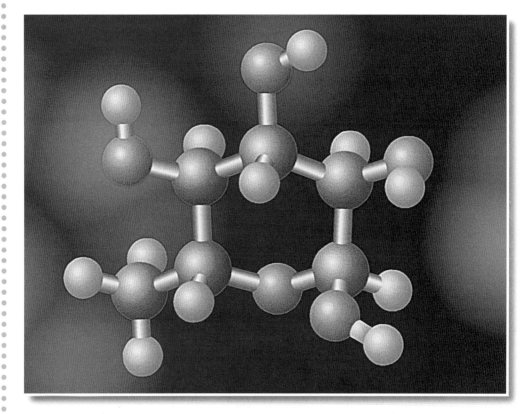

▲ *Glucose is built from 6 carbon, 12 hydrogen and 6 oxygen atoms.*

- **Glucose** is the body's energy chemical, used as the fuel in all cell activity.

- **Glucose is a kind of sugar** made by plants as they take energy from sunlight. It is commonly found in many fruits and fruit juices, along with fructose (see carbohydrates).

● **The body gets its glucose** from carbohydrates in food, broken down in stages in the intestine.

● **From the intestine,** glucose travels in the blood to the liver, where excess is stored in the form of starchy glycogen.

● **For the body to work effectively,** levels of glucose in the blood (called blood sugar) must always be correct.

● **Blood sugar levels** are controlled by two hormones, glucagon and insulin, sent out by the pancreas.

● **When blood sugar is low,** the pancreas sends out glucagon and this makes the liver change more glycogen to glucose.

● **When blood sugar is high,** the pancreas sends out insulin and this makes the liver store more glucose as glycogen.

● **Inside cells,** glucose may be burned for energy, stored as glycogen, or used to make triglyceride fats (see fats).

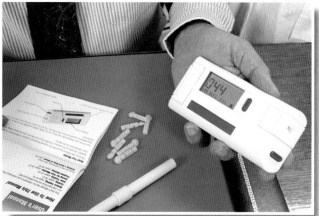

▶ *A blood glucose monitor checks that a person's blood sugar is at a healthy level.*

89

Carbohydrates

● **Carbohydrates** in food are your body's main source of energy. They are plentiful in sweet things and in starchy food such as bread, cakes and potatoes (see diet).

● **Carbohydrates** are burned by the body in order to keep it warm and to provide energy for growth and muscle movement, as well as to maintain basic body processes.

● **Carbohydrates** are among the most common of organic (life) substance – plants, for instance, make carbohydrates by taking energy from sunlight.

● **Carbohydrates** include chemical substances called sugars. Sucrose (the sugar in sugar lumps and caster sugar) is just one of these sugars.

● **Simple carbohydrates** such as glucose, fructose (the sweetness in fruit) and sucrose are sweet and soluble (they will dissolve in water).

● **Complex carbohydrates** (or polysaccharides) such as starch are made when molecules of simple carbohydrates join together.

▲ *Bread is especially rich in complex carbohydrates such as starch, as well as simpler ones such as glucose and sucrose.*

▲ *Carbohydrates give us the instant energy we need to help us lead a full and active life.*

- **A third type of carbohydrate** is cellulose (see diet).
- **The carbohydrates** you eat are turned into glucose for your body to use at once, or stored in the liver as the complex sugar glycogen (body starch).
- **The average adult** needs 2000 to 4000 Calories a day.
- **A Calorie** is the heat needed to warm 1 litre of water by 1°C.

Fats

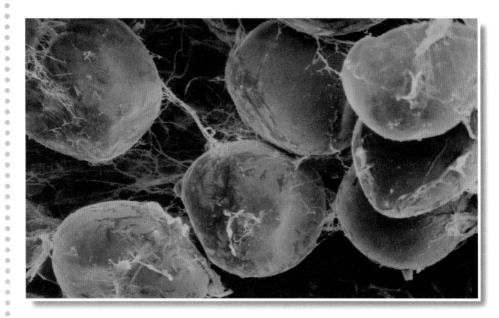

▲ *Fat cells are numerous under the skin, providing your body with a store of energy and a layer of insulation to keep you warm.*

- **Fats** are an important source of energy. Together with carbohydrates and proteins, they make up your body's three main components of foods.

- **While carbohydrates** are generally used for energy immediately, your body often stores fat to use for energy in times of shortage.

- **Weight for weight,** fats contain twice as much energy as carbohydrates.

- **Fats** are important organic (life) substances, found in almost every living thing. They are made from substances called fatty acids and glycerol.

- **Food fats** are greasy, vegetable or animal fats that will not dissolve in water.

- **Most vegetable fats** such as corn oil and olive oil are liquid, although some nut fats are solid.

- **Most animal fats,** as in meat, milk and cheese, are solid. Milk is mainly water with some solid animal fats. Most solid fats melt when warmed.

- **Fats called triglycerides** are stored around the body as adipose tissue (body fat). These act as energy stores and also insulate the body against the cold.

- **Fats called phospholipids** are used to build body cells.

- **In your stomach,** bile from your liver and enzymes from your pancreas break fats down into fatty acids and glycerol. These are absorbed into your body's lymphatic system or enter the blood.

◀ *Fats are either saturated or unsaturated. Cheese is a saturated fat. Saturated fats are linked to high levels of the substance cholesterol in the blood and may increase certain health risks, such as heart attack.*

Water

- **Your body** is mainly made of water – more than 60%.

- **You can survive weeks** without food, but no more than a few days without water.

- **You gain water** by drinking and eating, and as a by-product of cell activity.

- **You lose water** by sweating and breathing, and in your urine and faeces (see excretion).

- **The average person** takes in 2.2 litres of water a day – 1.4 litres in drink and 0.8 litres in food. Body cells add 0.3 litres, bringing the total water intake to 2.5 litres.

- **The average person** loses 1.5 litres of water every day in urine, 0.5 litres in sweat, 0.3 litres as vapour in the breath, and 0.2 litres in faeces.

- **The water balance** in the body is controlled mainly by the kidneys and adrenal glands.

▶ *Your body is mostly water. Even bone contains one-fifth water, while your brain is three-quarters water. You take it in through drinking and eating, and lose it by urinating, sweating and even breathing.*

- **The amount of water** the kidneys let out as urine depends on the amount of salt there is in the blood (see body salts).

- **If you drink a lot,** the saltiness of the blood is diluted (watered down). To restore the balance, the kidneys let out a lot of water as urine.

- **If you drink little** or sweat a lot, the blood becomes more salty, so the kidneys restore the balance by holding on to more water.

▶ *If you sweat a lot during heavy exercise, you need to make up for all the water you have lost by drinking. Your kidneys make sure that if you drink too much, you lose water as urine.*

95

Vitamins

- **Vitamins** are special substances the body needs to help maintain chemical processes inside cells.

- **Plants can make** their own vitamins, but humans must take most of their vitamins from food.

- **A lack of any vitamin** in the diet can cause certain illnesses.

- **Before the 18th century,** sailors on long voyages used to suffer the disease scurvy, caused by a lack in their diet of vitamin C from fresh fruit.

- **There are at least 15 vitamins** known.

◀ *Vegetables like these are rich in vitamins B and C, which is why we must eat plenty of them.*

96

▲ *This is a microscope photograph of a crystal of vitamin C, also known as ascorbic acid.*
This vitamin helps the body fight infections such as colds.

- **The first vitamins** discovered were given letter names like B. Later discoveries were given chemical names, such as E vitamins, which are known as tocopherols.

- **Some vitamins** such as A, D, E and K dissolve in fat and are found in animal fats and vegetable oils. They may be stored in the body for months.

- **Some vitamins** such as C and the Bs dissolve in water and are found in green leaves, fruits and cereal grains. They are used daily.

- **Vitamins D and K** are the only ones made in the body. Vitamin D is essential for bone growth in children.

97

Body salts

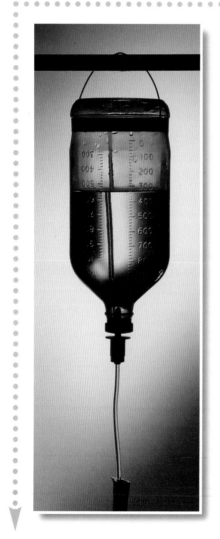

- **Body salts** are not simply the salt (sodium chloride) some people sprinkle on food – they are an important group of chemicals which play a vital role in your body.

- **Examples of components** in body salts include potassium, sodium, manganese, chloride, carbonate and phosphate.

- **Body salts are important** in maintaining the balance of water in the body, and on the inside and the outside of body cells.

- **The body's thirst centre** is the hypothalamus (see the brain). It monitors salt levels in the blood and sends signals telling the kidneys to keep water or to let it go.

- **You gain salt** in the food you eat.

- **You can lose salt** if you sweat heavily. This can make muscles cramp, which is why people take salt tablets in the desert or drink a weak salt solution.

- **Too much salt** in food may result in high blood pressure in certain people.

◄ *A saline drip is a salt solution injected via a tube into a patient who has lost blood.*

FASCINATING FACT
The kidneys control the amount of salts and water you have inside your body.

▲ *People who live in hot countries must eat plenty of salt on their food to make up for the loss of salt in their blood caused by continuous sweating.*

- **When dissolved in water,** the chemical elements that salt is made from split into ions – atoms or groups of atoms with either a positive or a negative electrical charge.

- **The balance** of water and salt inside and outside of body cells often depends on a balance of potassium ions entering the cell and sodium ions leaving it.

99

Osmosis and diffusion

- **To survive,** every living cell must constantly take in the chemicals it needs and let out the ones it does not need through its thin membrane (casing). Cells do this in several ways, including osmosis, diffusion and active transport.

- **Osmosis** is when water moves to even the balance between a weak solution and a stronger one.

- **Diffusion** is when the substances that are dissolved in water or mixed in air move to even the balance.

- **Osmosis happens** when the molecules of a dissolved substance are too big to slip through the cell membrane – only the water is able to move.

- **Osmosis is vital** to many body processes, including the workings of the kidney and the nerves.

- **Urine gets its water** from the kidneys by osmosis.

▲ *Water swallowed into the stomach passes through its lining into the blood, mainly by the process of osmosis.*

▲ *Like these jellyfish, every living cell must maintain the correct balance of chemicals inside and outside of them.*

● **In diffusion,** a substance such as oxygen moves in and out of cells, while the air or water it is mixed in mainly stays put.

● **Diffusion is vital** to body processes such as cellular respiration (see breathing), when cells take in oxygen and push out waste carbon dioxide.

● **Active transport** is the way a cell uses protein-based 'pumps' or 'gates' in its membrane to draw in and hold substances that might otherwise diffuse out.

● **Active transport** uses energy and is how cells draw in most of their food such as glucose.

101

Enzymes

- **Enzymes are** molecules that are mostly protein, and which alter the speed of chemical reactions in living things.

- **There are thousands of enzymes** inside your body – it would not be able to function without them.

- **Some enzymes** need an extra substance, called a coenzyme, to work. Many coenzymes are vitamins.

- **Most enzymes** have names ending in 'ase', such as lygase, protease and lipase.

- **Pacemaker enzymes** play a vital role in controlling your metabolism – the rate at which your body uses energy.

▲ *After you eat a meal, a complex series of enzymes gets to work, breaking the food down into the simple molecules that can be absorbed into your blood.*

- **One of the most important** enzyme groups is that of the messenger RNAs, which are used as communicators by the nuclei of body cells (see cells).

- **Many enzymes** are essential for the digestion of food, including lipase, protease, amylase, and the peptidases. Many of these enzymes are made in the pancreas.

▲ *From the moment you take your first bite of food, enzymes in your saliva begin to break carbohydrates down into glucose, preparing the food for digestion.*

- **Lipase is released** mainly from the pancreas into the alimentary canal (gut) to help break down fat.

- **Amylase breaks down starches** such as those in bread and fruit into simple sugars (see carbohydrates). There is amylase in saliva and in the stomach.

- **In the gut**, the sugars maltose, sucrose and lactose are broken down by maltase, sucrase and lactase.

Temperature

- **The inside of your body** stays at a constant temperature of 37°C (98°F), rising a few degrees only when you are ill.

- **Your body creates heat** by burning food in its cells, especially the 'energy sugar' glucose.

- **Even when you are resting,** your body generates so much heat that you are comfortable only when the air is slightly cooler than you are.

- **When you are working hard,** your muscles can generate as much heat as a 2 kW heater (a typical room heater).

- **Your body loses heat** as you breathe in cool air and breathe out warm air. Your body also loses heat by giving it off from your skin.

- **The body's temperature control** is the tiny hypothalamus in the lower front of the brain.

- **Temperature sensors** in the skin, in the body's core, and in the blood by the hypothalamus tell the hypothalamus how hot or cold your body is.

◀ *The body's temperature can be easily monitored using an electronic thermometer.*

▶ *A very hot day can sometimes make us feel uncomforatble. Splashing ourselves with cool water is often welcome relief!*

- **If it is too hot,** the hypothalamus sends signals to your skin telling it to sweat more. Signals also tell blood vessels in the skin to widen – this increases the blood flow, increasing the heat loss from your blood.

- **If it is too cold,** the hypothalamus sends signals to the skin to cut back skin blood flow, as well as signals to tell the muscles to generate heat by shivering.

- **If it is too cold,** the hypothalamus may also stimulate the thyroid gland to send out hormones to make your cells burn energy faster and so make more heat.

Excretion

▶ *To work well, your bowel needs plenty of roughage – the indigestible cellulose plant fibres found in food such as beans and wholemeal bread. Roughage keeps the muscles of the bowel properly exercised.*

● **Digestive excretion** is the way your body gets rid of food that it cannot digest.

● **Undigested food** is prepared for excretion in your large intestine or bowel.

● **The main part** of the large intestine is the colon, which is almost as long as you are tall.

● **The colon** converts the semi-liquid 'chyme' (see digestion) of undigested food into solid waste, by absorbing water.

● **The colon** soaks up 1.5 litres of water every day.

● **The colon walls** also absorb sodium and chlorine and get rid of bicarbonate and potassium.

● **Billions of bacteria** live inside the colon and help turn the chyme into faeces. These bacteria are harmless as long as they do not spread to the rest of the body.

● **Bacteria in the colon** make vitamins K and B – as well as smelly gases such as methane and hydrogen sulphide.

● **The muscles of the colon** break the waste food down into segments ready for excretion.

> ...FASCINATING FACT...
> About a third of all faeces is not old food
> but a mix of 'friendly' gut bacteria.

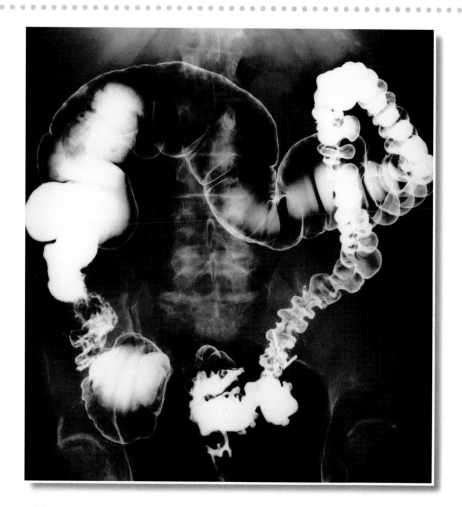

▲ *This is an X-ray of the colon. Patients drink a liquid called barium to enable their doctor to see the colon more clearly and check it is in working order.*

The kidneys

- **The kidneys** are a pair of bean-shaped organs inside the small of the back.

- **The kidneys** are the body's water control and blood-cleaning plants.

- **The kidneys** are high-speed filters that draw off water and important substances from the blood. They let unwanted water and waste substances go (see urine).

- **The kidneys filter** about 1.3 litres of blood a minute.

- **All the body's blood** flows through the kidneys every ten minutes, so blood is filtered 150 times a day.

- **The kidneys manage** to recycle or save every re-useable substance from the blood. They take 85 litres of water and other blood substances from every 1000 litres of blood, but only let out 0.6 litres as urine.

- **The kidneys** save nearly all the amino acids and glucose (see diet) from the blood and 70% of the salt.

- **Blood entering each kidney** is filtered through a million or more filtration units called nephrons.

- **Each nephron** is an incredibly intricate network of little pipes called convoluted tubules, wrapped around countless tiny capillaries. Useful blood substances are filtered into the tubules, then re-absorbed back into the blood in the capillaries.

- **Blood enters each nephron** through a little cup called the Bowman's capsule via a bundle of capillaries.

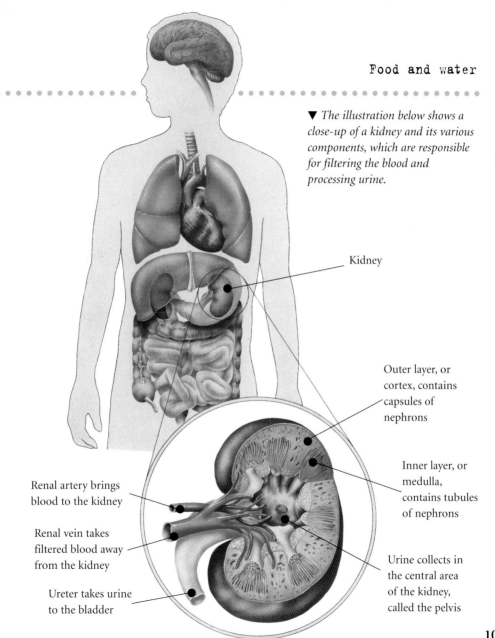

▼ *The illustration below shows a close-up of a kidney and its various components, which are responsible for filtering the blood and processing urine.*

Kidney

Outer layer, or cortex, contains capsules of nephrons

Inner layer, or medulla, contains tubules of nephrons

Renal artery brings blood to the kidney

Renal vein takes filtered blood away from the kidney

Ureter takes urine to the bladder

Urine collects in the central area of the kidney, called the pelvis

109

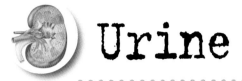

Urine

- **Urine** is one of your body's ways of getting rid of waste (see water).

- **Your kidneys** produce urine, filtering it from your blood.

- **Urine runs from** each kidney down a long tube called the ureter, to a bag called the bladder.

- **Your bladder fills** up with urine over several hours. When it is full, you feel the need to urinate.

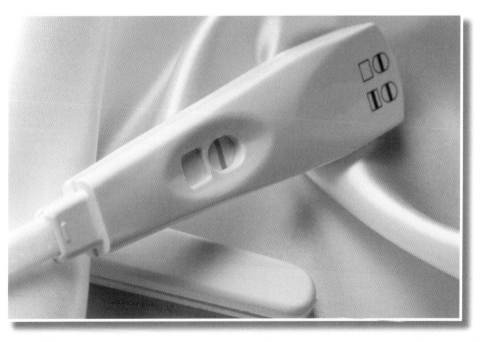

▲ *Urine can be used to test for pregnancy. A woman may use a home pregnancy test kit (above) to check her urine for a particular hormone, which, if present, will mean she is pregnant.*

- **Urine is mostly water**, but there are substances dissolved in it. These include urea, various salts, creatinine, ammonia and blood wastes.

- **Urea** is a substance that is left after the breakdown of amino acids (see diet).

- **Urine gets its smell** from substances such as ammonia.

- **Urine gets its colour** from a yellowish blood waste called urochrome. Urochrome is left after proteins are broken down.

- **If you sweat a lot** – perhaps during a fever – your kidneys will let less water go and your urine will be stronger in colour.

▲ *Doctors can get clues to illnesses by testing what substances there are in urine. Diabetes, for instance, is shown up by the presence of glucose in the urine.*

...FASCINATING FACT...
During your life you will urinate 45,000 litres – enough to fill a small swimming pool!

The immune system

The adenoids in the nose are one of the body's defence centres, releasing cells to fight infections

If you get a throat infection the tonsils release cells to fight it

The thymus is a gland in the chest which turns ordinary white blood cells into special T-cells that fight harmful microbes

During an infection, lymph nodes may swell up with white blood cells that have swallowed up germs

The spleen not only destroys worn-out red blood cells, but also helps make antibodies and phagocytes

◀ *The body's range of interior defences against infection is amazingly complex. The various kinds of white blood cells and the antibodies the defences make are particularly important.*

Lymph glands in the groin often swell up as the body fights an infection

Sebaceous glands in the skin ooze an oil that is poisonous to many bacteria

▶ *The AIDS virus, HIV, attacks the body's immune cells and prevents them dealing with infections.*

112

- **The immune system** is the complicated system of defences that your body uses to prevent or fight off attack from germs and other invaders.

- **Your body** has a variety of barriers, toxic chemicals and booby traps to stop germs entering it. The skin is a barrier that stops many germs getting in, as long as it is not broken.

- **Mucus is a thick, slimy fluid** that coats vulnerable, internal parts of your body such as your stomach and nose. It also acts as a lubricant (oil), making swallowing easier.

- **Mucus lines your airways** and lungs to protect them from smoke particles as well as from germs. Your airways may fill up with mucus when you have a cold, as your body tries to minimize the invasion of airborne germs.

- **Itching, sneezing, coughing and vomiting** are your body's ways of getting rid of unwelcome invaders. Small particles that get trapped in the mucous lining of your airways are wafted out by tiny hairs called cilia.

- **The body** has many specialized cells and chemicals which fight germs that get inside you.

- **Complement** is a mixture of liquid proteins found in the blood which attacks bacteria.

- **Interferons** are proteins which help the body's cells to attack viruses and also stimulate killer cells (see lymphocytes).

- **Certain white blood cells** are cytotoxic, which means that they are poisonous to invaders.

- **Phagocytes** are big white blood cells that swallow up invaders and then use an enzyme to dissolve them (see antibodies). They are drawn to the site of an infection whenever there is inflammation.

113

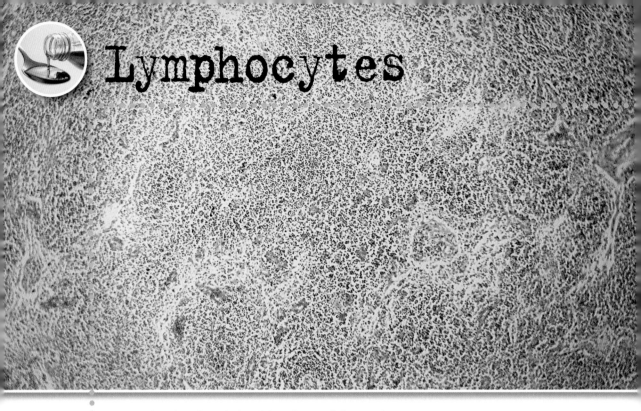

Lymphocytes

▲ *A lymph node packed with lymphocytes fighting infection.*

- **Lymphocytes** are white blood cells that play a key role in the body's immune system, which targets invading germs.

- **There are two kinds of lymphocyte** – B lymphocytes (B-cells) and T lymphocytes (T-cells).

- **B-cells** develop into plasma cells that make antibodies to attack bacteria such as those which cause cholera, as well as some viruses (see antibodies).

- **T-cells** work against viruses and other micro-organisms that hide inside body cells. T-cells help identify and destroy these invaded cells or their products. They also attack certain bacteria.

- **There are two kinds of T-cell** – killers and helpers.

- **Helper T-cells** identify invaded cells and send out chemicals called lymphokines as an alarm, telling killer T-cells to multiply.

- **Invaded cells** give themselves away by abnormal proteins on their surface.

- **Killer T-cells** lock on to the cells that have been identified by the helpers, then move in and destroy them.

- **Some B-cells**, called memory B-cells, stay around for a long time, ready for a further attack by the same organism.

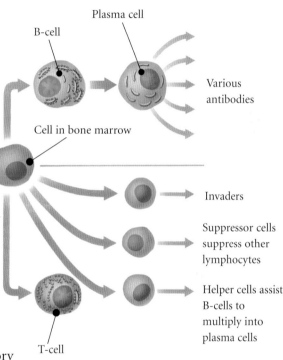

B-cell

Plasma cell

Various antibodies

Cell in bone marrow

Invaders

Suppressor cells suppress other lymphocytes

Helper cells assist B-cells to multiply into plasma cells

T-cell

▲ *Our bodies are constantly under attack from harmful bacteria and viruses. Lymphocytes are key defenders, producing special cells to either identify, alert, suppress or kill.*

> ...FASCINATING FACT...
> If you get flu, it is your T lymphocytes that come to the rescue and fight off the virus.

115

Antibodies

- **Antibodies** are tiny proteins that make germs vulnerable to attack by white blood cells called phagocytes (see the immune system).

- **Antibodies are produced** by white blood cells derived from B lymphocyctes (see lymphocytes).

- **There are thousands** of different kinds of B-cell in the blood, each of which produces antibodies against a particular germ.

- **Normally, only a few B-cells** carry a particular antibody. But when an invading germ is detected, the correct B-cell multiplies rapidly to cause the release of antibodies.

- **Invaders** are identified when your body's immune system recognizes proteins on their surface as foreign. Any foreign protein is called an antigen.

▲ *Pollen can often cause allergies like hayfever. Your immune system mistakenly produces antibodies to fight the harmless pollen grains, causing an allergic reaction.*

▶ *Bacteria, viruses and many other micro-organisms have antigens which spur B-cells into action to produce antibodies, as this artist's impression shows.*

- **Your body was armed** from birth with antibodies for germs it had never met. This is called innate immunity.

- **If your body comes across** a germ it has no antibodies for, it quickly makes some. It then leaves memory cells ready to be activated if the germ invades again. This is called acquired immunity.

- **Acquired immunity** means you only suffer once from some infections, such as chickenpox. This is also how vaccination works.

- **Allergies** are sensitive reactions that happen in your body when too many antibodies are produced, or when they are produced to attack harmless antigens.

- **Autoimmune diseases** are ones in which the body forms antibodies against its own tissue cells.

117

Vaccination

- **Vaccination** helps to protect you against an infectious disease by exposing you to a mild or dead version of the germ in order to make your body build up protection in the form of antibodies.

- **Vaccination** is also called immunization, because it builds up your resistance or immunity to a disease.

- **In passive immunization** you are injected with substances such as antibodies which have already been exposed to the germ. This gives instant but short-lived protection.

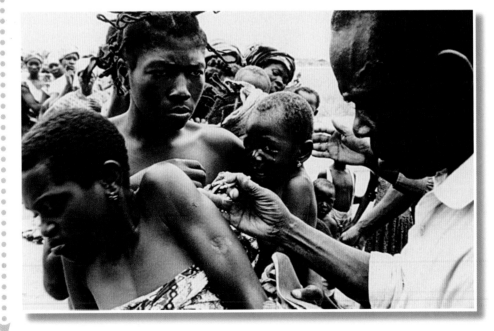

▲ *Vaccinations are crucial in many tropical regions where diseases are more widespread.*

- **In active immunization** you are given a killed or otherwise harmless version of the germ. Your body makes the antibodies itself for long-term protection.

- **Children in many countries** are given a series of vaccinations as they grow up, to protect them against diseases such as diphtheria, tetanus and polio.

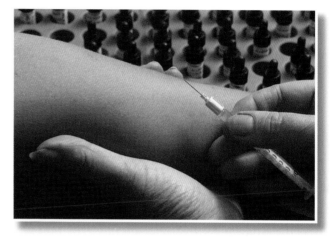

▲ *Diseases such as diphtheria, rubella and whooping cough are now rare in many countries thanks to vaccination. The dangerous disease smallpox – once very common – has been wiped out.*

- **The measles vaccine** carries a 1-in-87,000 chance of causing encephalitis (brain inflammation).

- **In cholera, typhoid, rabies and flu vaccines,** the germ in the vaccine is killed to make it harmless.

- **In measles, mumps, polio and rubella vaccines,** the germ is live attenuated – this means that its genes or other parts have been altered in order to make it harmless.

- **In diphtheria and tetanus vaccines,** the germ's toxins (poisons) are removed to make them harmless.

- **The hepatitis B** vaccine can be prepared by genetic engineering.

119

Hormones

- **Hormones are** the body's chemical messengers, released from stores at times to trigger certain reactions in different parts of the body.

- **Most hormones** are endocrine hormones which are spread around your body in your bloodstream.

- **Each hormone** is a molecule with a certain shape that creates a certain effect on target cells.

- **Hormones are controlled** by feedback systems. This means they are only released when their store gets the right trigger – which may be a chemical in the blood or another hormone.

- **Major hormone sources** include: the pituitary gland just below the brain; the thyroid gland; the adrenal glands; the pancreas; a woman's ovaries; a man's testes.

▶ *During an exhilarating moment, adrenalin boosts your breathing and heartbeat, and makes your skin sweat and eyes widen.*

- **The pituitary** is the source of many important hormones, including growth hormones which spur growing.

- **Adrenaline** is released by the adrenals to ready your body for action.

- **Endorphins and enkephalins** block or relieve pain.

- **Oestrogen and progesterone** are female sex hormones that control a woman's monthly cycle.

- **Testosterone** is a male sex hormone which controls the workings of a man's sex organs.

▲ *Women over the age of around 45 to 55 stop producing some female hormones.*

The thyroid gland

- **The thyroid** is a small gland about the size of two joined cherries. It is situated at the front of your neck, just below the larynx (see airways and vocal cords).

- **The thyroid** secretes (releases) three important hormones – tri-iodothyronine (T3), thyroxine (T4) and calcitonin.

- **The thyroid hormones** affect how energetic you are by controlling your metabolic rate.

- **Your metabolic rate** is the rate at which your body cells use glucose.

▶ *The thyroid is part of your energy control system, telling your body cells to work faster or slower in order to keep you warm or to make your muscles work harder.*

...FASCINATING FACT...
The thyroid hormone, calcitonin, controls
the amount of calcium in the blood.

- **T3 and T4** control metabolic rate by circulating into the blood and stimulating cells to convert more glucose.

- **If the thyroid** sends out too little T3 and T4, you get cold and tired, your skin gets dry and you put on weight.

- **If the thyroid** sends out too much T3 and T4, you get nervous, sweaty and overactive, and you lose weight.

- **The amount of T3 and T4** sent out by the thyroid depends on how much thyroid-stimulating hormone is sent to it from the pituitary gland (see the brain).

- **If the levels of T3 and T4** in the blood drop, the pituitary gland sends out extra thyroid-stimulating hormone to tell the thyroid to produce more.

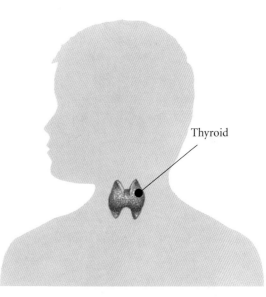

Thyroid

▲ *The thyroid gland is usually described as the size and shape of a bow tie, and is even situated in the same place.*

123

Sex hormones

- **The sexual development** of girls and boys depends on the sex hormones (see reproduction).

- **Sex hormones** control the development of primary and secondary sexual characteristics, and regulate all sex-related processes such as sperm and egg production.

- **Primary sexual characteristics** are the development of the major sexual organs, in particular the genitals.

- **Secondary sexual characteristics** are other differences between the sexes, such as men's beards.

- **There are three main types of sex hormone** – androgens, oestrogen and progesterone.

▶ *A girl's sexual development depends on female sex hormones.*

▶ *Men grow facial hair due to the male sex hormone, testosterone.*

● **Androgens** are male hormones such as testosterone. They make a boy's body develop features such as a beard, deepen his voice and make his penis grow.

● **Oestrogen** is the female hormone made mainly in the ovaries. It not only makes a girl develop her sexual organs, but controls her monthly menstrual cycle.

● **Progesterone** is the female hormone that prepares a girl's uterus (womb) for pregnancy every month.

● **Some contraceptive pills** have oestrogen in them to prevent the ovaries releasing their egg cells.

...FASCINATING FACT...
Boys have female sex hormones and girls male sex hormones, but they usually have no effect.

125

The eye

- **Your eyes** are tough balls that are filled with a jelly-like substance called vitreous humour.

- **The cornea** is a thin, glassy dish across the front of your eye. It allows light rays through the eye's window, the pupil, and into the lens.

- **The iris** is the coloured, muscular ring around the pupil. The iris narrows in bright light and widens when light is dim.

- **The lens** is just behind the pupil. It focuses the picture of the world on to the back of the eye.

- **The back of the eye** is lined with millions of light-sensitive cells. This lining is called the retina, and it registers the picture and sends signals to the brain via the optic nerve.

- **There are two kinds** of light-sensitive cell in the retina – rods and cones. Rods are very sensitive and work in even dim light, but they cannot detect colours. Cones respond to colour.

- **Some kinds of cone** are very sensitive to red light, some to green and some to blue. One theory says that the colours we see depend on how strongly they affect each of these three kinds of cone (see colour vision).

- **Each of your two eyes** gives you a slightly different view of the world. The brain combines these views to give an impression of depth and 3-D solidity.

- **Although each eye** gives a slightly different view of the world, we see things largely as just one eye sees it. This dominant eye is usually the right eye.

> ...FASCINATING FACT...
> The picture received by your retina looks large and real –
> yet it is upside down and just a few millimetres across.

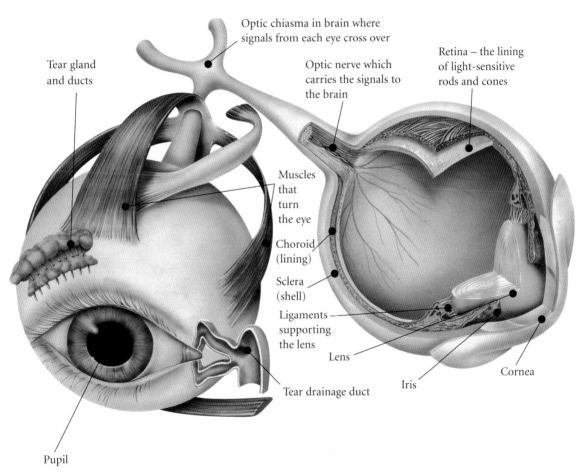

Optic chiasma in brain where signals from each eye cross over

Tear gland and ducts

Optic nerve which carries the signals to the brain

Retina – the lining of light-sensitive rods and cones

Muscles that turn the eye

Choroid (lining)

Sclera (shell)

Ligaments supporting the lens

Lens

Tear drainage duct

Iris

Cornea

Pupil

▲ *This illustration shows your two eyeballs, with a cutaway to reveal the cornea and lens (which projects light rays through the eye's window) and the light-sensitive retina (which registers it).*

127

Colour vision

▲ *Seeing all the colours of the world around you depends on the colour-sensitive cone cells inside your eyes.*

● **Seeing in colour** depends on eye cells called cones.

● **Cones do not** work well in low light, which is why things seem grey at dusk.

● **Some cones** are more sensitive to red light, some are more sensitive to green and some to blue.

● **The old trichromatic theory** said that you see colours by comparing the strength of the signals from each of the three kinds of cone – red, green and blue.

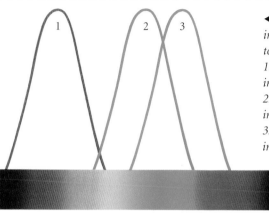

◀ *Three different types of cone in the human eye are each sensitive to a different part of the spectrum:*
1. Sensitivity of the red cone peaks in the red part of the spectrum.
2. Sensitivity of the green cone peaks in the green part of the spectrum.
3. Sensitivity of the blue cone peaks in the blue part of the spectrum.

White light spectrum

- **The trichromatic theory** does not explain colours such as gold, silver and brown.

- **The opponent-process theory** said that you see colours in opposing pairs – blue and yellow, red and green.

- **In opponent-process theory,** lots of blue light is thought to cut your awareness of yellow, and vice versa. Lots of green cuts your awareness of red, and vice versa.

- **Now scientists** combine these theories and think that colour signals from the three kinds of cone are further processed in the brain in terms of the opposing pairs.

- **Ultraviolet light** is light waves too short for you to see, although some birds and insects can see it.

... FASCINATING FACT ...
You have over 5 million colour-detecting cones in the retina of each eye.

The ear

- **Pinnae** (singular, pinna) are the ear flaps you can see on the side of your head, and they are simply collecting funnels for sounds.

- **A little way inside your head,** sounds hit a thin, tight wall of skin, called the eardrum, making it vibrate.

- **When the eardrum vibrates,** it shakes three little bones called ossicles. These are the smallest bones in the body.

- **The three ossicle bones** are the malleus (hammer), the incus (anvil) and the stapes (stirrup).

- **When the ossicles vibrate,** they rattle a tiny membrane called the oval window, intensifying the vibration.

- **The oval window** is 30 times smaller in area than the eardrum.

- **Beyond the oval window** is the cochlea – a winding collection of three, liquid-filled tubes, which looks a bit like a snail shell.

- **In the middle tube** of the cochlea there is a flap which covers row upon row of tiny hairs. This is called the organ of Corti.

- **When sounds make** the eardrum vibrate, the ossicles tap on the oval window, making pressure waves shoot through the liquid in the cochlea and wash over the flap of the organ of Corti, waving it up and down.

- **When the organ of Corti waves,** it tugs on the tiny hairs under the flap. These send signals to the brain via the auditory nerve, and you hear a sound.

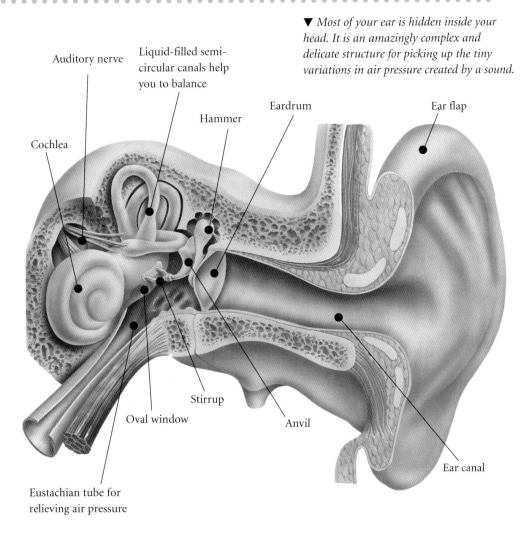

▼ *Most of your ear is hidden inside your head. It is an amazingly complex and delicate structure for picking up the tiny variations in air pressure created by a sound.*

Auditory nerve

Liquid-filled semi-circular canals help you to balance

Hammer

Eardrum

Ear flap

Cochlea

Stirrup

Oval window

Anvil

Ear canal

Eustachian tube for relieving air pressure

131

Balance

- **To stay upright,** your body must send a continual stream of data about its position to your brain – and your brain must continually tell your body how to move to keep its balance.

- **Balance** is controlled in many parts of the brain, including the brain's cerebellum.

- **Your brain** finds out about your body position from many sources, including your eyes, proprioceptors around the body, and the semicircular canals and other chambers in the inner ear.

▶ *To stop you losing your balance, it helps to fix your eyes on a single focal point, so that your brain does not become confused or distracted.*

▲ *A rollercoaster ride can make you feel dizzy because the liquid inside your inner ear keeps spinning after you have stopped.*

- **Proprioceptors** are sense receptors in your skin, muscles and joints (see co-ordination).

- **The semicircular canals** are three, tiny, fluid-filled loops in your inner ear (see the ear).

- **Two chambers** (holes) called the utricle and saccule are linked to the semicircular canals.

- **When you move your head,** the fluid in the canals and cavities lags a little, pulling on hair detectors which tell your brain what is going on.

- **The canals** tell you whether you are nodding or shaking your head, and which way you are moving.

- **The utricle and saccule** tell you if you tilt your head or if its movement speeds up or slows down.

133

Smell

- **Smells are scent molecules** which are taken into your nose by breathed-in air. A particular smell may be noticeable even when just a single scent molecule is mixed in with millions of air molecules.

- **The human nose** can tell the difference between more than 10,000 different chemicals.

- **Dogs can pick up** smells that are 10,000 times fainter than the ones humans can detect.

- **Inside the nose,** scent molecules are picked up by a patch of scent-sensitive cells called the olfactory epithelium.

- **Olfactory** means 'to do with the sense of smell'.

- **The olfactory epithelium** contains over 25 million receptor cells.

▲ *Scents are closely linked to emotions in the brain, and perfume can be a powerful way of triggering feelings.*

- **Each of the receptor cells** in the olfactory epithelium has up to 20 or so scent-detecting hairs called cilia.

- **When they are triggered** by scent molecules, the cilia send signals to a cluster of nerves called the olfactory bulb, which then sends messages to the part of the brain that recognizes smell.

- **The part of the brain** that deals with smell is closely linked to the parts that deal with memories and emotions. This may be why smells can often evoke vivid memories.

- **By the age of 20,** you will have lost 20% of your sense of smell. By 60, you will have lost 60% of it.

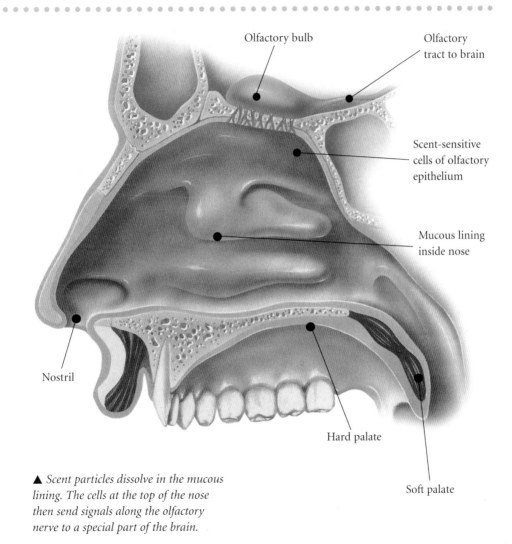

Olfactory bulb

Olfactory tract to brain

Scent-sensitive cells of olfactory epithelium

Mucous lining inside nose

Nostril

Hard palate

Soft palate

▲ *Scent particles dissolve in the mucous lining. The cells at the top of the nose then send signals along the olfactory nerve to a special part of the brain.*

135

Taste

▲ *As well as tasting the flavour of ice cream, the tongue can also tell that it is cold and smooth.*

- **The sense of taste** is the crudest of our five senses, giving us less information about the world than any other sense.

- **Taste** is triggered by certain chemicals in food, which dissolve in the saliva in your mouth, and then send information to a particular part of the brain via sensory nerve cells on the tongue.

136

▶ *Certain parts of the tongue are more sensitive to one flavour than to others, as shown in this diagram.*

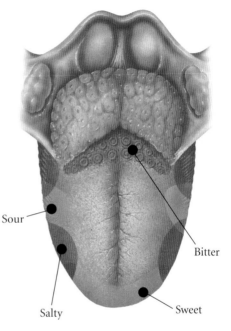

Sour

Bitter

Salty

Sweet

- **Taste buds** are receptor cells found around tiny bumps called papillae on the surface of your tongue.

- **Taste buds** are sensitive to four basic flavours: sweet, sour, bitter and salty.

- **The back of the tongue** contains big round papaillae shaped like an upside-down V. This is where bitter flavours are sensed.

- **The front of the tongue** is where fungiform (mushroom-like) papillae and filiform (hairlike) papillae carry taste buds that detect sweet, sour and salty flavours.

- **As well as taste,** the tongue can also feel the texture and temperature of food.

- **Your sense of taste** works closely together with your sense of smell to make the flavour of food more interesting.

- **Strong tastes,** such as spicy food, rely less on the sense of smell than on pain-sensitive nerve endings in the tongue.

- **People can learn** to distinguish more flavours and tastes than normal, as is the case with tea- or wine-tasters.

137

Touch

- **Touch,** or physical contact, is just one of the five sensations that are spread all over your body in your skin. The others include pressure, pain, hot and cold.

- **There are sense receptors** everywhere in your skin, but places like your face have more than your back.

- **There are 200,000** hot and cold receptors in your skin, plus 500,000 touch and pressure receptors, and nearly 3 million pain receptors.

- **Free nerve-endings** are rather like the bare end of a wire. They respond to all five kinds of skin sensation and are almost everywhere in your skin.

- **There are specialized receptors** in certain places, each named after their discoverer.

▲ *The fingertips are where your sense of touch is most sensitive.*

> **....FASCINATING FACT...**
> Your brain knows just how hard you are touched from how fast nerve signals arrive.

▲ *As we grow up, we gradually learn to identify more and more things instantly through touch.*

- **Pacini's corpuscles** and Meissner's endings react instantly to sudden pressure.

- **Krause's bulbs**, Merkel's discs and Ruffini's endings respond to steady pressure.

- **Krause's bulbs** are also sensitive to cold.

- **Ruffini's endings** also react to changes in temperature.

Co-ordination

▲ *Dancing of any kind tests the body's balance and co-ordination to its limits.*

● **Co-ordination** means balanced or skilful movement.

● **To make you move,** your brain has to send signals out along nerves telling all the muscles involved exactly what to do.

● **Co-ordination of the muscles** is handled by the cerebellum at the back of your brain (see the brain).

- **The cerebellum** is given instructions by the brain's motor cortex (see the cortex).

- **The cerebellum sends** its commands via the basal ganglia in the middle of the brain.

- **Proprioceptors** are nerve cells that are sensitive to movement, pressure or stretching. Proprioceptor means 'one's own sensors'.

- **Proprioceptors are all over your body** – in muscles, tendons and joints – and they all send signals to your brain telling it the position or posture of every part of your body.

- **The hair cells** in the balance organs of your ear are also proprioceptors (see balance).

▲ *Ball skills demand incredible muscle co-ordination, relying on high-speed signals sent from the brain.*

· · · FASCINATING FACT · · ·
Proprioceptors allow you to touch forefingers behind your back.

The nervous system

- **The nervous system** is your body's control and communication system, made up of nerves and the brain. Nerves are your body's hot-lines, carrying instant messages from the brain to every organ and muscle – and sending back an endless stream of data to the brain about what is going on both inside and outside your body.

- **The central nervous system** (CNS) is the brain and spinal cord (see central nervous system).

▲ A spider has a nervous system with about 100,000 nerve cells, while a human being has around 60 billion.

- **The peripheral nervous system** (PNS) is made up of the nerves that branch out from the CNS to the rest of the body.

- **The main branches of the PNS** are the 12 cranial nerves in the head, and the 31 pairs of spinal nerves that branch off the spinal cord.

- **The nerves of the PNS** are made up of long bundles of nerve fibres, which in turn are made from the long axons (tails) of nerve cells, bound together like the wires in a telephone cable.

142

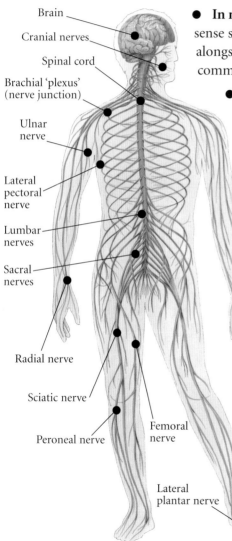

Brain

Cranial nerves

Spinal cord

Brachial 'plexus' (nerve junction)

Ulnar nerve

Lateral pectoral nerve

Lumbar nerves

Sacral nerves

Radial nerve

Sciatic nerve

Peroneal nerve

Femoral nerve

Lateral plantar nerve

● **In many places**, sensory nerves (which carry sense signals from the body to the brain) run alongside motor nerves (which carry the brain's commands telling muscles to move).

● **Some PNS nerves** are as wide as your thumb. The longest is the sciatic, which runs from the base of the spine to the knee.

● **The autonomic nervous system** (ANS) is the body's third nervous system. It controls all internal body processes such as breathing automatically, without you even being aware of it.

● **The ANS** is split into two complementary (balancing) parts – the sympathetic and the parasympathetic. The sympathetic system speeds up body processes when they need to be more active, such as when the body is exercising or under stress. The parasympathetic slows them down.

◀ The nervous system is an incredibly intricate network of nerves linking your brain to every part of the body. The nerves of the peripheral nervous system branch out to every limb and body part from the central nervous system (the brain and spinal cord).

143

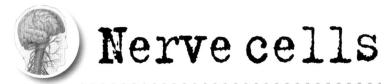

Nerve cells

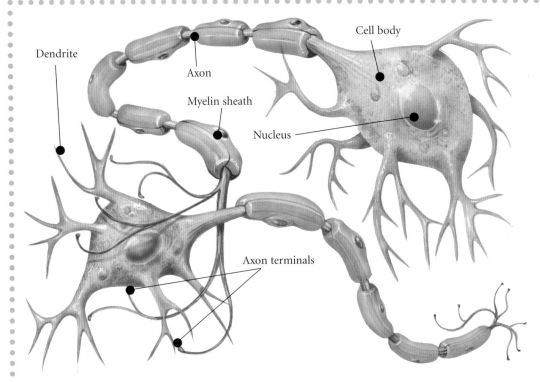

Dendrite

Axon

Myelin sheath

Cell body

Nucleus

Axon terminals

▲ *Nerve cells, or neurons, are the 'wires' of the body's nervous system. They carry messages within, to and from the central nervous system along fine branches called dendrites and long tails called axons.*

- **Nerves** are made of very specialized cells called neurons.

- **Neurons** are spider-shaped with a nucleus at the centre, lots of branching threads called dendrites, and a winding tail called an axon which can be up to 1 m long.

- **Axon terminals** on the axons of one neuron link to the dendrites or body cell of another neuron.

- **Neurons link up** like beads on a string to make your nervous system.

- **Most cells are** short-lived and are constantly being replaced by new ones. Neurons, however, are very long-lived – some are never actually replaced after you are born.

- **Nerve signals** travel as electrical pulses, each pulse lasting about 0.001 seconds.

- **When nerves are resting** there are extra sodium ions with a positive electrical charge on the outside of the nerve cell, and extra negative ions inside.

- **When a nerve fires,** little gates open in the cell wall all along the nerve, and positive ions rush in to join the negative ions. This makes an electrical pulse.

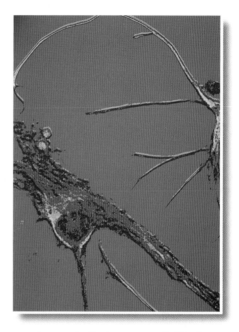

▲ *Microscopically tiny nerve cells like this were first seen when stained with silver nitrate by the Italian scientist Camillo Golgi in the 1870s.*

- **Long-distance nerves** are insulated (covered) by a sheath of a fatty substance, myelin, to keep the signal strong.

- **Myelinated (myelin-sheathed) nerves** shoot signals through very fast – at more than 100 metres per second.

- **Ordinary nerves** send signals at about 1 to 2 metres per second.

145

Synapses

◀ Our changes of mood can be caused by imbalances of the neurotransmitter, serotonin, in our nervous system.

- **Synapses** are the very tiny gaps between nerve cells.

- **When a nerve signal** goes from one nerve cell to another, it must be transmitted (sent) across the synapse by special chemicals called neurotransmitters.

- **Droplets of neurotransmitter** are released into the synapse whenever a nerve signal arrives.

- **As the droplets of neurotransmitter** lock on to the receiving nerve's receptors, they fire the signal onwards.

- **Each receptor site** on a nerve-ending only reacts to certain neurotransmitters. Others have no effect.

- **Sometimes** several signals must arrive before enough neurotransmitter is released to fire the receiving nerve.

- **More than 40 neurotransmitter chemicals** have been identified.

- **Dopamine** is a neurotransmitter that works in the parts of the brain that control movement and learning. Parkinson's disease may develop when the nerves that produce dopamine break down.

- **Serotonin** is a neurotransmitter that is linked to sleeping and waking up, and also to your mood.

- **Acetylcholine** is a neurotransmitter that may be involved in memory, and also in the nerves that control muscle movement.

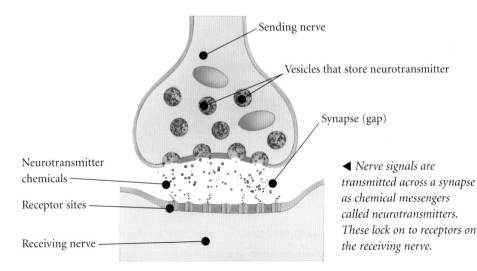

Sending nerve

Vesicles that store neurotransmitter

Synapse (gap)

Neurotransmitter chemicals

Receptor sites

Receiving nerve

◀ *Nerve signals are transmitted across a synapse as chemical messengers called neurotransmitters. These lock on to receptors on the receiving nerve.*

147

Sensory nerves

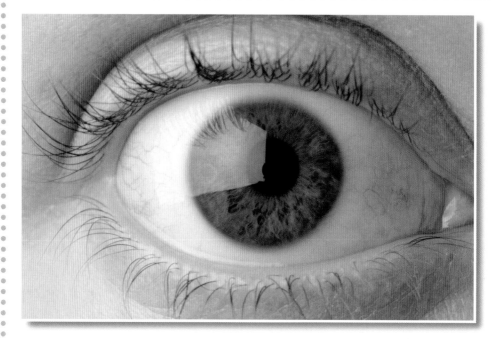

▲ *Sight is the sense most people rely on above all the others.*

● **Sensory nerves** are the nerves that carry information to your brain from sense receptors all over your body.

● **Each sense receptor** in the body is linked to the brain by a sensory nerve.

● **Most sensory nerves** feed their signals to the somatosensory cortex, which is the strip situated around the top of the brain where sensations are registered (see the cortex).

● **Massive bundles** of sensory nerve cells form the nerves that link major senses such as the eyes, ears and nose to the brain.

▶ *Some of our most pleasant feelings, such as being hugged or stroked, are sent to the brain by sensory nerves.*

- **The eyes are linked to the brain** by the optic nerves.

- **The ears are linked to the brain** by the auditory nerves.

- **The nose is linked to the brain** by the olfactory tracts.

- **In the skin**, many sense receptors are simply 'free' – meaning they are exposed sensory nerve-endings.

- **The sciatic nerve** to each leg is the longest nerve in the body. Its name is from the Latin for 'pain in the thigh'.

- **We can tell** how strong a sensation is by how fast the sensory nerve fires signals to the brain. But no matter how strong the sensation is, the nerve does not go on firing at the same rate and soon slows down.

149

- **Motor nerves** are connected to your muscles and tell your muscles to move.

- **Each major muscle** has many motor nerve-endings that instruct it to contract (tighten).

- **Motor nerves cross over** from one side of your body to the other at the top of your spinal cord. This means that signals from the right side of your brain go to the left side of your body, and vice versa.

- **Each motor nerve** is paired to a proprioceptor on the muscle and its tendons (see co-ordination). This sends signals to the brain to say whether the muscle is tensed or relaxed.

- **If the strain** on a tendon increases, the proprioceptor sends a signal to the brain. The brain adjusts the motor signals to the muscle so it contracts more or less.

- **Motor nerve signals** originate in a part of the brain called the motor cortex (see the cortex).

- **All the motor nerves** (apart from those in the head) branch out from the spinal cord.

- **The gut** has no motor nerve-endings but plenty of sense endings, so you can feel it but cannot move it consciously.

- **The throat** has motor nerve-endings but few sense endings, so you can move it but not feel it.

- **Motor neuron disease** is a disease that attacks motor nerves within the central nervous system.

◀ *Motor nerves fire signals to the muscles to make them move to hit the ball.*

151

Central nervous system

- **The central nervous system** (CNS) is made up of the brain and the spinal cord (the nerves of the spine).

- **The CNS** contains billions of densely packed interneurons – nerve cells with very short connecting axons (see nerve cells).

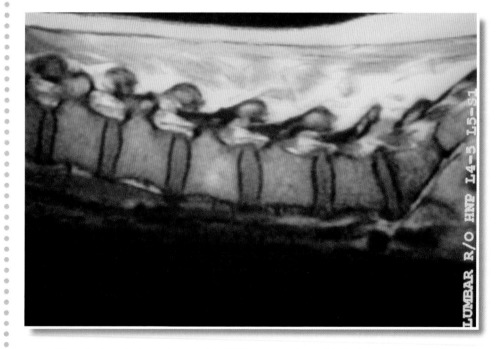

LUMBAR R/O HNP L4-5 L5-S1

▲ *The spinal cord, shown here in this CAT scan, together with the brain and nerves, form the body's central information system, making sure all its different parts work together efficiently.*

> . . . FASCINATING FACT . . .
> The CNS sends out messages to more
> than 640 muscles around the body.

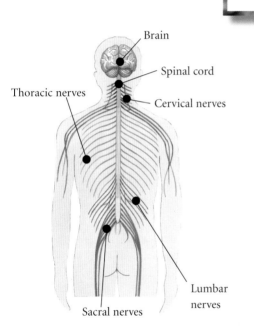

Brain

Spinal cord

Thoracic nerves

Cervical nerves

Lumbar
nerves

Sacral nerves

▲ *Spinal nerves branch off the spinal cord
in pairs, with one nerve on either side.
They are arranged in four groups, and
there is one pair between each of the
neighbouring 32 vertebrae.*

- **The CNS is cushioned** from damage by a surrounding bath of liquid called cerebrospinal fluid.

- **There are 86 main nerves** branching off the CNS.

- **There are 12 pairs of cranial nerves,** and 31 pairs of spinal nerves.

- **Cranial nerves** are the 12 pairs of nerves that branch off the CNS out of the brain.

- **Spinal nerves** are the 31 pairs of nerves that branch off the spinal cord.

- **The spinal nerves** are made up of 8 cervical nerve pairs, 12 thoracic pairs, 5 lumbar pairs, 5 sacral pairs and one coccyx pair.

- **Many spinal nerves** join up just outside the spine in five spaghetti junctions called plexuses.

The spinal cord

- **The spinal cord** is the bundle of nerves running down the middle of the backbone.

- **The spinal cord** is the route for all nerve signals travelling between the brain and the body.

- **The spinal cord** can actually work independently of the brain, sending out responses to the muscles directly.

- **The outside** of the spinal cord is made of the long tails or axons of nerve cells and is called white matter; the inside is made of the main nerve bodies and is called grey matter.

- **Your spinal cord** is about 43 cm long and 1 cm thick. It stops growing when you are about five years old.

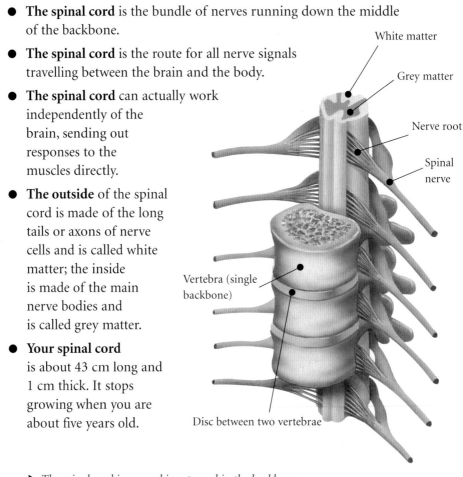

White matter

Grey matter

Nerve root

Spinal nerve

Vertebra (single backbone)

Disc between two vertebrae

▶ *The spinal cord is encased in a tunnel in the backbone at the back of each vertebra. Nerves branch off to the body in pairs either side.*

- **Damage to the spinal cord** can cause paralysis.

- **Injuries below the neck** can cause paraplegia – paralysis below the waist.

- **Injuries to the neck** can cause quadriplegia – paralysis below the neck.

- **Descending pathways** are groups of nerves that carry nerve signals down the spinal cord – typically signals from the brain for muscles to move.

- **Ascending pathways** are groups of nerves that carry nerve signals up the spinal cord – typically signals from the skin and internal body sensors going to the brain.

◄ *When the spinal cord gets damaged, nerves cannot carry messages from the brain to the muscles to tell the body to move. This is called paraplegia, or paralysis below the waist, and means the person will be unable to walk.*

The brain

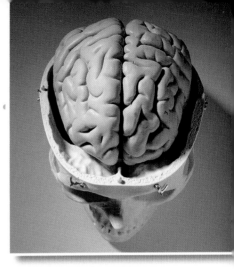

▲ *Taking the top off the skull shows the brain to be a soggy, pinky-grey mass which looks rather like a giant walnut.*

- **The human brain** is made up of more than 100 billion nerve cells called neurons.

- **Each neuron** is connected to as many as 25,000 other neurons – so the brain has trillions and trillions of different pathways for nerve signals.

- **Girls' brains** weigh 2.5% of their body weight, on average, while boys' brains weigh 2%.

- **About 0.85 litres** of blood shoots through your brain every minute. The brain may be as little as 2% of your body weight, but it demands 12 – 15% of your blood supply.

- **An elephant's brain** weighs four times as much as the human brain. Some apes, monkeys and dolphins are quite near our brain–body ratio.

- **The cerebral cortex** is the outside of the brain, and if it was laid out flat, it would cover a bed.

- **The left hemisphere (half)** of the upper part of the brain is more dominant in speech, writing and general language, the right half in pictures and ideas.

- **Conscious thoughts and actions** happen in the cerebral cortex.

- **A human brain** has a cerebral cortex four times as big as a chimpanzee, about 20 times as big as a monkey's, and about 300 times as big as a rat's.

- **Unconscious, automatic activities** such as breathing, hunger, sleep and so on are controlled by structures such as the hypothalamus and the brain stem.

...**FASCINATING FACT**...
Scientists can now grow human brain cells in a laboratory dish.

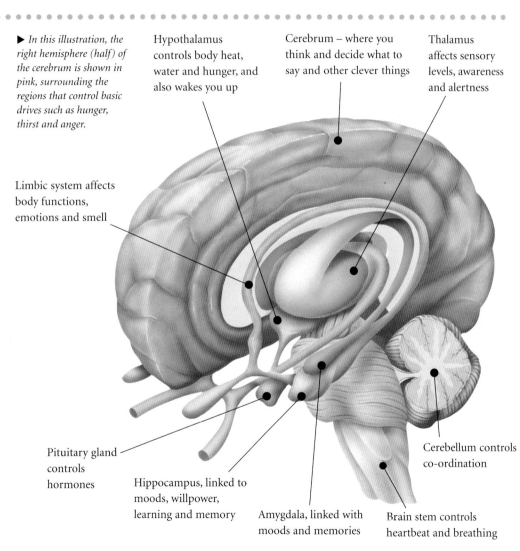

▶ *In this illustration, the right hemisphere (half) of the cerebrum is shown in pink, surrounding the regions that control basic drives such as hunger, thirst and anger.*

Hypothalamus controls body heat, water and hunger, and also wakes you up

Cerebrum – where you think and decide what to say and other clever things

Thalamus affects sensory levels, awareness and alertness

Limbic system affects body functions, emotions and smell

Pituitary gland controls hormones

Hippocampus, linked to moods, willpower, learning and memory

Amygdala, linked with moods and memories

Brain stem controls heartbeat and breathing

Cerebellum controls co-ordination

157

The cortex

- **A cortex** is the outer layer of any organ, such as the brain or the kidney.

- **The brain's cortex** is also known as the cerebral cortex. It is a layer of interconnected nerve cells around the outside of the brain, called 'grey matter'.

- **The cerebral cortex** is where many signals from the senses are registered in the brain.

- **The visual cortex** is around the lower back of the brain. It is the place where all the things you see are registered in the brain.

- **The somatosensory cortex** is a band running over the top of the brain like a headband. This where a touch on any part of the body is registered.

- **The motor cortex** is a band just in front of the sensory cortex. It sends out signals to body muscles to move.

- **The more nerve ending**s there are in a particular part of the body, the more of the sensory cortex it occupies.

- **The lips and face** take up a huge proportion of the sensory cortex.

- **The hands** take up almost as much of the sensory cortex as the face.

▶ *The cortex is only 5 mm thick, but flattened out would cover an area almost as big as an office desk, and contains at least 50 billion nerve cells.*

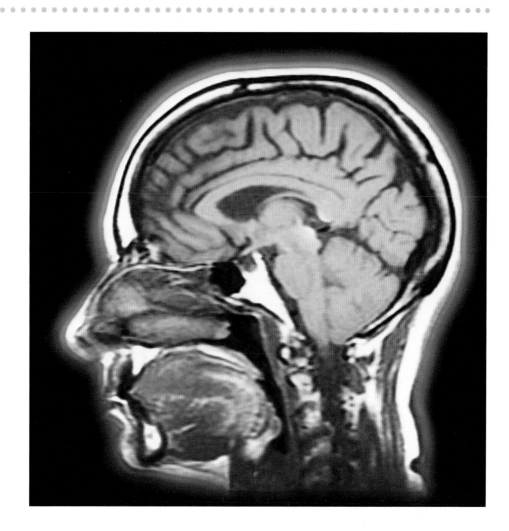

Sleeping

- **When you are asleep,** many of your body functions go on as normal – even your brain goes on receiving sense signals. But your body may save energy and do routine repairs.

- **Lack of sleep** can be dangerous. A newborn baby needs 18 to 20 hours sleep a day. An adult needs around 7 to 8.

- **Sleep is controlled** in the brain stem (see the brain). Dreaming is stimulated by signals fired from a part of the brain stem called the pons.

▲ *The traditional tale of Rip Van Winkle tells of how he fell into a deep sleep for 20 years. When he finally woke up, he couldn't understand why the world was so different.*

- **When you are awake,** there is little pattern to the electricity created by the firing of the brain's nerve cells. But as you sleep, more regular waves appear.

- **While you are asleep,** alpha waves sweep across the brain every 0.1 seconds. Theta waves are slower.

◄ *We all shut our eyes to sleep. Other marked changes to the body include the pattern of the brain's activity, relaxation of skeletal muscles, reduced urine production and slower heartbeat, breathing and digestive activity.*

- **For the first 90 minutes** of sleep, your sleep gets deeper and the brain waves become stronger.

- **After about 90 minutes** of sleep, your brain suddenly starts to buzz with activity, yet you are hard to wake up.

- **After 90 minutes** of sleep, your eyes begin to flicker from side to side under their lids. This is called Rapid Eye Movement (REM) sleep.

- **REM sleep** is thought to show that you are dreaming.

- **While you sleep**, ordinary deeper sleep alternates with spells of REM lasting up to half an hour.

Mood

- **Mood is** your state of mind – whether you are happy or sad, angry or afraid, overjoyed or depressed.

- **Moods and emotions** seem to be strongly linked to the structures in the centre of the brain, where unconscious activities are controlled (see the brain).

- **Moods** have three elements – how you feel, what happens to your body, and what moods make you do.

- **Some scientists** think the way you feel causes changes in the body – you are happy so you smile, for example.

- **Other scientists** think changes in the body alter the way you feel – smiling makes you happy.

▶ *The reasons why we react the way we do in certain situations, such as feeling happy, is still unclear to scientists. But emotions like these are what make us unique as human beings.*

> ...**FASCINATING FACT**...
> In one experiment, people injected with adrenaline found rotten jokes much funnier!

- **Yet other scientists** think moods start automatically – before you even know it – when something triggers off a reaction in the thalamus in the centre of the brain.

- **The thalamus** then sends mood signals to the brain's cortex and you become aware of the mood.

- **The thalamus** also sets off automatic changes in the body through the nerves and hormones.

- **Certain memories or experiences** are so strongly linked in your mind that they can often automatically trigger a certain mood.

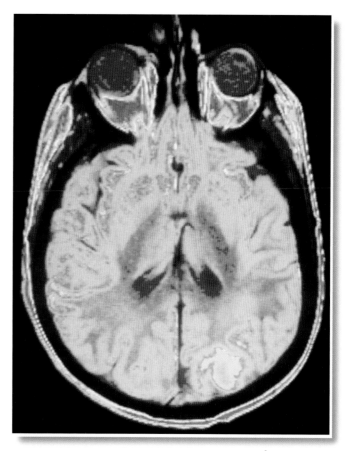

▲ *Scientists are only just beginning to discover how moods and emotions are linked to particular parts of the brain.*

Thinking

- **Some scientists** claim that we humans are the only living things that are conscious, meaning that we alone are actually aware that we are thinking.

- **No one knows** how consciousness works – it is one of science's last great mysteries.

- **Most of your thoughts** seem to take place in the cerebrum (at the top of your brain), and different kinds of thought are linked to different areas, called association areas.

- **Each half of the cerebrum** has four rounded ends called lobes – two at the front, called frontal and temporal lobes, and two at the back, called occipital and parietal lobes.

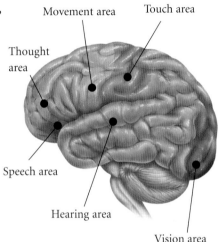

Movement area Touch area

Thought area

Speech area

Hearing area

Vision area

▲ *The 'thought' area at the front of the brain helps us to think, solve problems and be creative.*

- **The frontal lobe** is linked to your personality and it is where you have your bright ideas.

- **The temporal lobe** is where you hear and understand what people are saying to you.

- **The occipital lobe** is where you work out what your eyes see.

- **The left half of the brain** (left hemisphere) controls the right side of the body. The right half (right hemisphere) controls the left side.

▶ *Modern scanning techniques have taught us a great deal about the human brain and brain processes by allowing us to see brains in action.*

- **One half of the brain** is always dominant (in charge). Usually, the left brain is dominant, which is why 90% of people are right-handed.
- **The parietal lobe** is where you register touch, heat and cold, and pain.

165

Memory

▲ *Special moments like birthday parties lead to long-lasting memories.*

● **When you remember** something, your brain probably stores it by creating new nerve connections.

● **You have** three types of memory – sensory, short-term and long-term.

● **Sensory memory** is when you go on feeling a sensation for a moment after it stops.

● **Short-term memory** is when the brain stores things for a few seconds, like a phone number you remember long enough to press the buttons.

- **Long-term memory** is memory that can last for months or maybe even your whole life.

- **Your brain** seems to have two ways of remembering things for the long term. Scientists call these two different ways declarative and non-declarative memories.

- **Non-declarative memories** are skills you teach yourself by practising, such as playing badminton or the flute. Repetition establishes nerve pathways.

- **Declarative memories** are either episodic or semantic. Each may be sent by the hippocampus region of the brain to the correct place in the cortex, the brain's wrinkly outer layer where you do most of your thinking.

▲ *Learning to play the violin involves non-declarative memory – in which nerve pathways become reinforced by repeated use. This is why practising is so important.*

- **Episodic memories** are memories of striking events in your life, such as breaking your leg or your first day at a new school. You not only recall facts, but sensations.

- **Semantic memories** are facts such as dates. The brain seems to store these in the left temporal lobe, at the front left-hand side of your brain.

167

Chromosomes

- **Chromosomes** are the microscopically tiny, twisted threads inside every cell that carry your body's life instructions in chemical form.

- **There are 46 chromosomes** in each of your body cells, divided into 23 pairs.

- **One of each chromosome pair** came from your mother and the other from your father.

- **In a girl's 23 chromosome pairs,** each half exactly matches the other (the set from the mother is equivalent to the set from the father).

- **Boys** have 22 matching chromosome pairs, but the 23rd pair is made up of two odd chromosomes.

- **The 23rd chromosome pair** decides what sex you are, and the sex chromosomes are called X and Y.

▶ *A girl turns out to be a girl because she gets an X chromosome from her father. A boy gets a Y chromosome from his father.*

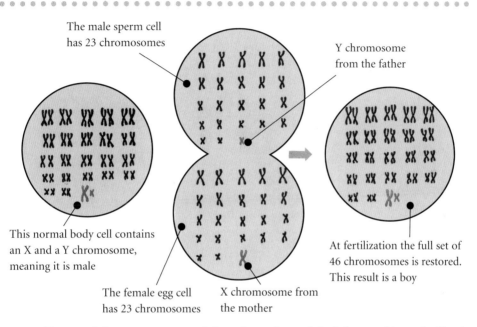

The male sperm cell
has 23 chromosomes

Y chromosome
from the father

This normal body cell contains
an X and a Y chromosome,
meaning it is male

At fertilization the full set of
46 chromosomes is restored.
This result is a boy

The female egg cell
has 23 chromosomes

X chromosome from
the mother

▲ *Two sets of chromosomes, one each from the mother and the father, combine at fertilization.*

- **Girls have two X chromosomes,** but boys have an X and a Y chromosome.

- **In every matching pair,** both chromosomes give your body life instructions for the same thing.

- **The chemical instructions** on each chromosome come in thousands of different units called genes.

- **Genes for the same feature** appear in the same locus (place) on each matching pair of chromosomes in every human body cell. Scientists one day hope to find out how the entire pattern, called the genome, works.

Genes

DNA coiled into a chromosome

'Rungs' made from four
different chemical bases

DNA's double
spiral shape,
like a twisted
rope ladder

DNA
unravelling

Chromosome
in miniature

The new copy,
called RNA, is
used to make the
proteins

Each of these bases will pair
up with only one other base

Strands of DNA
dividing to make
a template

◀ DNA (Deoxyribonucleic Acid) is
the tiny molecule inside every cell
that carries all your genes in a
code – the genetic code. Most of the
time, DNA is coiled up inside the
chromosomes, but when needed, it
unravels its double helix (corkscrew)
shape, like a twisted ladder. Four
chemical bases make up the 'rungs' of this
ladder. Each base pairs with only one other,
so the sequence of bases along one strand of the
DNA is a perfect mirror image of the sequence
on the other side. When the strand divides down
the middle, each can be used like a template to
make a copy. This is how instructions are issued.

- **Genes** are the body's chemical instructions for your entire life – for growing up, surviving, having children and, perhaps, even for dying.

- **Individual genes** are instructions to make particular proteins – the body's building-block molecules.

- **Small sets of genes** control features such as the colour of your hair or your eyes, or create a particular body process such as digesting fat from food.

- **Each of your body cells** (except egg and sperm cells) carries identical sets of genes. This is because all your cells were made by other cells splitting in two, starting with the original egg cell in your mother.

- **Your genes are a mixture** – half come from your mother and half from your father (see chromosomes). But none of your brothers or sisters will get the same mix, unless you are identical twins.

- **Genes make us unique** – making us tall or short, fair or dark, brilliant dancers or speakers, healthy or likely to get particular illnesses, and so on.

- **Genes are sections** of DNA – a microscopically tiny molecule inside each cell.

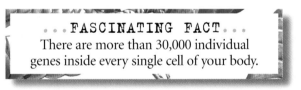

. . . FASCINATING FACT . . .
There are more than 30,000 individual genes inside every single cell of your body.

- **DNA** is shaped in a double helix with linking bars, like a twisted rope ladder.

- **The bars of DNA** are four special chemicals called bases – guanine, adenine, cytosine and thymine.

- **The bases in DNA** are set in groups of three called codons, and the order of the bases in each codon varies to provide a chemical code for the cell to make a particular amino acid.

Heredity

▲ *Sisters tend to look alike, as they have inherited similar genes from their parents.*

- **Your heredity** is all the body characteristics you inherit from your parents, whether it is your mother's black hair or your father's knobbly knees.

- **Characteristics** are passed on by the genes carried on your chromosomes.

- **The basic laws** of heredity were discovered by the Austrian monk Gregor Mendel 150 years ago.

- **Your body characteristics** are a mix of two sets of instructions – one from your mother's chromosomes and the other from your father's.

- **Each characteristic** is the work of only one gene – either your mother's or your father's. This gene is said to be 'expressed'.

- **A gene that is not expressed** does not vanish. Instead, it stays dormant (asleep) in your chromosomes, possibly to pass on to your children.

- **A gene** that is always expressed is called a dominant gene.

- **A recessive gene** is one that loses out to a dominant gene and stays dormant.

- **A recessive gene** may be expressed when there is no competition – that is, when the genes from both of your parents are recessive.

▲ *The gene for blue eyes is recessive, but if a girl gets a blue-eye gene from both of her parents, she may have blue eyes.*

Reproduction– female

- **A woman's reproductive system** is where her body stores, releases and nurtures the egg cells (ova – singular, ovum) that create a new human life when joined with a male sperm cell.

- **All the egg cells** are stored from birth in the ovaries – two egg-shaped glands inside the pelvic region. Each egg is stored in a tiny sac called a follicle.

- **One egg cell** is released every monthly menstrual cycle by one of the ovaries.

- **A monthly menstrual cycle starts** when follicle-stimulating hormone (FSH) is sent by the pituitary gland in the brain to spur follicles to grow.

- **As follicles grow,** they release the sex hormone oestrogen. Oestrogen makes the lining of the uterus (womb) thicken.

- **When an egg is ripe,** it slides down a duct called a Fallopian tube.

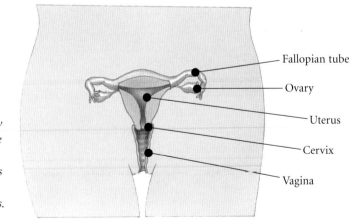

▶ *This is a frontal view of the inside of a female reproductive system, showing the two ovaries and Fallopian tubes, which join to the uterus.*

Fallopian tube

Ovary

Uterus

Cervix

Vagina

- **If a woman** has sexual intercourse at this time, sperm from the man's penis may swim up her vagina, enter her womb and fertilize the egg in the Fallopian tube.

- **If the egg is fertilized,** the womb lining goes on thickening ready for pregnancy, and the egg begins to develop into an embryo.

- **If the egg is not fertilized,** it is shed with the womb lining in a flow of blood from the vagina. This shedding is called a menstrual period.

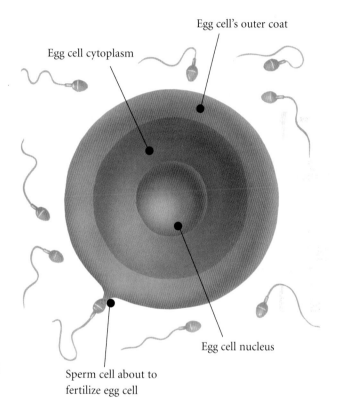

Egg cell's outer coat

Egg cell cytoplasm

Egg cell nucleus

Sperm cell about to fertilize egg cell

▲ *The female egg cell passes along the woman's Fallopian tube. At fertilization, tiny sperm cells swarm around the egg until one sperm manages to push its head on to the surface of the egg. The sperm head and egg membrane join, and fertilization takes place.*

175

Reproduction – male

- **A boy or man's reproductive system** is where his body creates the sperm cells that combine with a female egg cell to create a new human life.

- **Sperm cells** look like microscopically tiny tadpoles. They are made in the testes, which is inside the scrotum.

- **The testes and scrotum** hang outside the body where it is cooler, because this improves sperm production.

- **At 15**, a boy's testes can make 200 million sperm a day.

- **Sperm leave** the testes via the epididymis – a thin, coiled tube, about 6 m long.

Acrosome cap

Sperm head

Nucleus with genetic material

Midsection

Sperm tail

▲ *A mature sperm cell consists of a head, where the genetic information is stored, a midsection and a tadpole-like tail, which allows it to swim rapidly towards the female egg cell.*

- **When the penis** is stimulated during sexual intercourse, sperm are driven into a tube called the vas deferens and mix with a liquid called seminal fluid to make semen.

- **Semen** shoots through the urethra (the tube inside the penis through which males urinate) and is ejaculated into the female's vagina.

- **The male sex hormone** testosterone is also made in the testes.

- **Testosterone** stimulates bone and muscle growth.

- **Testosterone** also stimulates the development of male characteristics such as facial hair and a deeper voice.

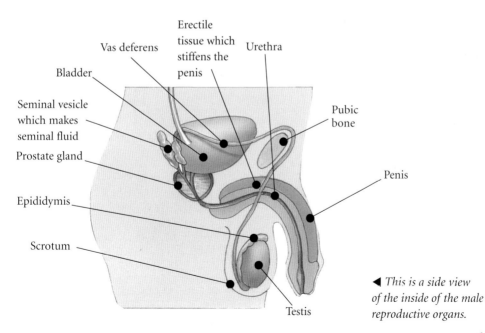

Erectile tissue which stiffens the penis

Vas deferens

Urethra

Bladder

Seminal vesicle which makes seminal fluid

Prostate gland

Epididymis

Scrotum

Pubic bone

Penis

Testis

◀ *This is a side view of the inside of the male reproductive organs.*

177

Pregnancy

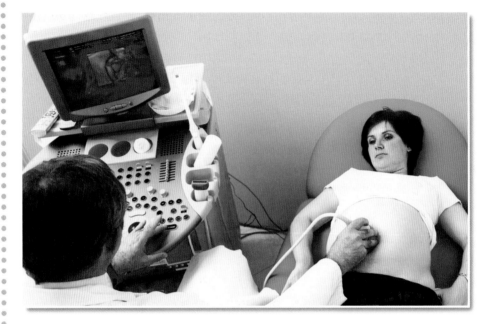

▲ *At different stages during her pregnancy, a woman has at least one ultrasound scan to check that the foetus is healthy and growing as it should.*

- **Pregnancy** begins when a woman's ovum (egg cell) is fertilized by a man's sperm cell. Usually this happens after sexual intercourse, but it can begin in a laboratory.

- **When a woman becomes pregnant** her monthly menstrual periods stop. Tests on her urine show whether she is pregnant.

- **During pregnancy,** the fertilized egg divides again and again to grow rapidly – first to an embryo (the first eight weeks), and then to a foetus (from eight weeks until birth).

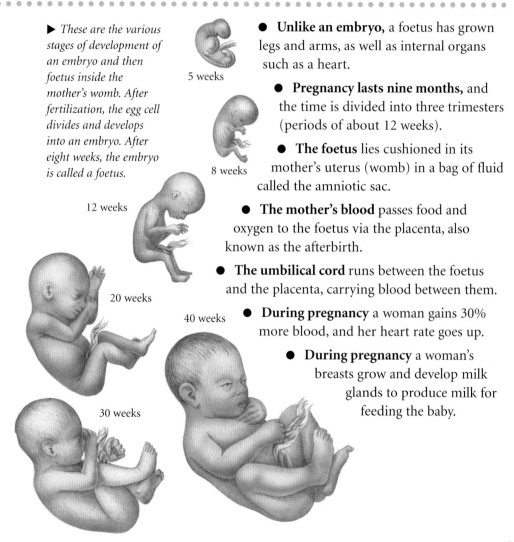

▶ *These are the various stages of development of an embryo and then foetus inside the mother's womb. After fertilization, the egg cell divides and develops into an embryo. After eight weeks, the embryo is called a foetus.*

5 weeks

8 weeks

12 weeks

20 weeks

40 weeks

30 weeks

● **Unlike an embryo,** a foetus has grown legs and arms, as well as internal organs such as a heart.

● **Pregnancy lasts nine months,** and the time is divided into three trimesters (periods of about 12 weeks).

● **The foetus** lies cushioned in its mother's uterus (womb) in a bag of fluid called the amniotic sac.

● **The mother's blood** passes food and oxygen to the foetus via the placenta, also known as the afterbirth.

● **The umbilical cord** runs between the foetus and the placenta, carrying blood between them.

● **During pregnancy** a woman gains 30% more blood, and her heart rate goes up.

● **During pregnancy** a woman's breasts grow and develop milk glands to produce milk for feeding the baby.

179

Birth

- **Babies are usually born** 38–42 weeks after the mother becomes pregnant.

- **A few days or weeks before a baby is born,** it usually turns in the uterus (womb) so its head is pointing down towards the mother's birth canal (her cervix and vagina).

- **Birth begins** as the mother goes into labour – when the womb muscles begin a rhythm of contracting (tightening) and relaxing in order to push the baby out through the birth canal.

- **There are three stages** of labour. In the first, the womb muscles begin to contract or squeeze, bursting the bag of fluid around the baby. This is called breaking the waters.

▼ *A mother makes a special bond with her baby.*

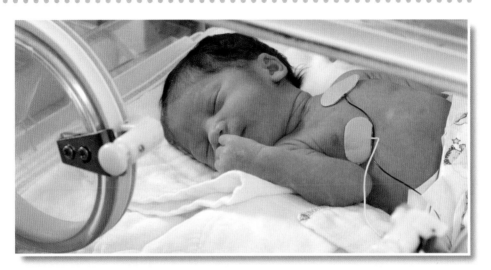

▲ *Babies that weigh below 2.4 kg are known as premature, and are nursed in special care units.*

- **In the second stage** of labour, the baby is pushed out through the birth canal, usually by its head first, the body following quite quickly.

- **In the third stage** of labour, the placenta, which passed oxygen and nutrients from the mother's blood, is shed and comes out through the birth canal.

- **The umbilical cord** is the baby's lifeline to its mother. It is cut after birth.

- **A premature baby** is one born before it is fully developed.

- **A miscarriage** is when the developing baby is 'born' before the 28th week of pregnancy and cannot survive.

- **A Caesarian section** is an operation that happens when a baby cannot be born through the birth canal and emerges from the womb through a surgical cut made in the mother's belly.

181

Babies

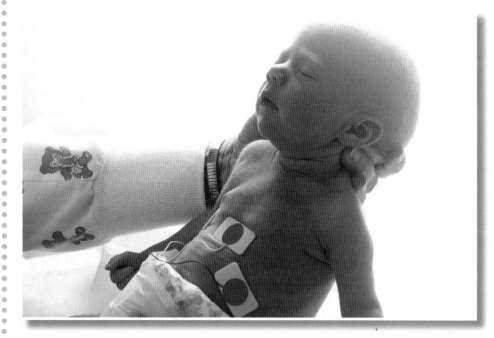

▲ *A newborn baby's muscles cannot hold up its head, so it must be supported.*

- **A baby's head** is three-quarters of the size it will be as an adult
  – and a quarter of its total body height.

- **The bones** of a baby's skeleton are fairly soft, to allow for growth.
  They harden over time.

- **Baby boys grow faster** than baby girls during the first seven months.

- **A baby** has a very developed sense of taste, with
  taste buds all over the inside of its mouth.

182

...FASCINATING FACT...
A baby's brain is one of the fastest-
growing parts of its body.

- **Babies have** a much stronger sense of smell than adults – perhaps to help them find their mother.

- **There are two gaps** called fontanelles between the bones of a baby's skull, where there is only membrane (a 'skin' of thin tissue), not bone. The gaps close and the bones join together by about 18 months.

- **A baby is born** with primitive reflexes (things it does automatically) such as grasping or sucking a finger.

- **A baby's body weight** usually triples in the first year of its life.

- **A baby seems to learn** to control its body in stages, starting first with its head, then moving on to its arms and legs.

▶ *Babies start to crawl when their leg muscles grow strong enough, after nine months or so.*

Puberty

- **Puberty** is the time of life when girls and boys mature sexually.

- **The age of puberty varies hugely,** but on average it is between 10 and 13 years for girls, and between 11 and 15 years for boys.

- **Puberty is started** by two hormones sent out by the pituitary gland (see the brain) – the follicle-stimulating hormone and the luteinizing hormone.

- **During puberty, a girl** will develop breasts and grow hair under her arms and around her genitals.

- **Inside her body,** a girl's ovaries grow ten times as big and release sex hormones (see reproduction – female).

- **The sex hormones** oestrogen and progesterone spur the development of a girl's sexual organs and control her monthly menstrual cycle.

▶ *In their early teens, girls go through puberty and begin to develop the sexual characteristics that will make them women.*

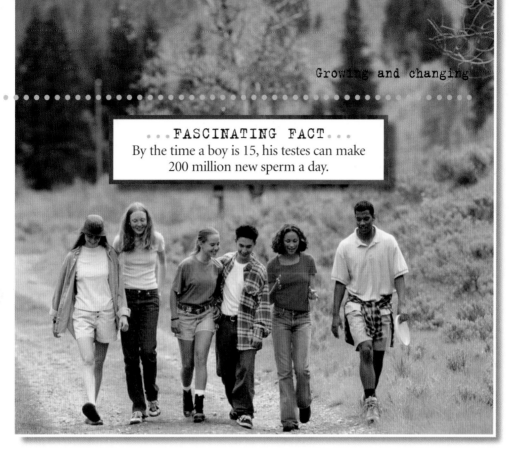

▲ *Puberty is part of the longer and more complex time called adolescence, when young people start to change, not only physically, but in the way they think and behave as well.*

- **A year or so after puberty begins,** a girl has her menarche (the first menstrual period). When her periods come regularly, she will be able to have a baby.

- **For a boy during puberty,** his testes grow and hair sprouts on his face, under his arms and around his genitals (see reproduction - male).

- **Inside his body,** a boy's testes begin to make sperm.

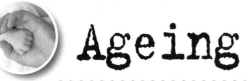

Ageing

▲ *People in Japan have a long life expectancy. This is probably due to a combination of factors including a healthy diet and certain social customs, which tend to favour the elderly.*

● **Most people live** for between 60 and 100 years, although a few live even longer than this.

● **The longest officially confirmed age** is that of Frenchwoman Jeanne Calment, who died in 1997, aged 122 years and 164 days.

● **Life expectancy** is how long statistics suggest you are likely to live.

- **On average in Europe**, men can expect to live about 75 years and women about 80. However, because health is improving generally, people are now living longer.

- **As adults grow older**, their bodies begin to deteriorate (fail). Senses such as hearing, sight and taste weaken.

- **Hair goes grey** as pigment (colour) cells stop working.

- **Muscles weaken** as fibres die.

- **Bones become more brittle** as they lose calcium. Cartilage shrinks between joints, causing stiffness.

- **Skin wrinkles** as the rubbery elastin and collagen fibres that support it sag. Exposure to sunlight speeds this up, which is why the face and hands get wrinkles first.

- **Circulation and breathing weaken**. Blood vessels may become stiff and clogged, forcing the heart to work harder and raising blood pressure.

▲ *Changes in health standards mean that more and more people than ever before are remaining fit in old age.*

187

Diagnosis

- **Diagnosis** is when a doctor works out what a patient is suffering from – the illness and perhaps its cause.

- **The history** is the patient's own account of their illness. This provides the doctor with a lot of clues.

- **The prognosis** is the doctor's assessment of how the illness will develop in the future.

- **Symptoms** are changes which the patient or others notice and report.

- **Signs** are changes the doctor detects on examination and maybe after tests.

- **After taking a history** the doctor may carry out a physical examination, looking at the patient's body for symptoms such as swelling and tenderness.

▼ *A doctor examines her patient to check for any swelling or abnormalities that will help her make a diagnosis.*

▲ *To make a diagnosis, a doctor may need to carry out a number of different tests. One such test involves taking the patient's blood pressure.*

- **A stethoscope** is a set of ear tubes which allows the doctor to listen to the body sounds, such as breathing and the heart beating.

- **With certain symptoms,** a doctor may order laboratory tests of blood and urine samples. Devices such as ultrasounds and X-rays may also be used to take special pictures.

- **Doctors** nowadays may use computers to help them make a diagnosis.

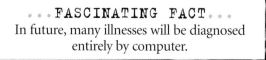

...FASCINATING FACT...
In future, many illnesses will be diagnosed
entirely by computer.

189

Disease

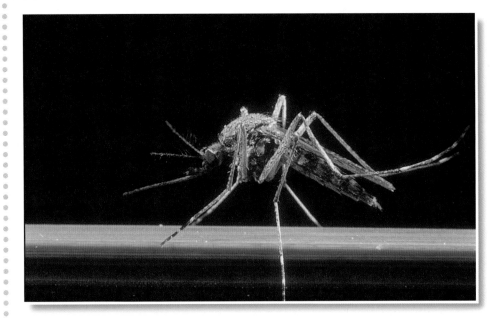

▲ *Mosquitos spread deadly diseases by transferring infected blood from one person to another.*

- **A disease** is something that upsets the normal working of any living thing. It can be acute (sudden, but short-lived), chronic (long-lasting), malignant (spreading) or benign (not spreading).

- **Some diseases** are classified by the body part they affect (such as heart disease), or by the body activity they affect (such as respiratory, or breathing, disease).

- **Heart disease** is the most common cause of death in the USA, Europe and also Australia.

- **Some diseases** are classified by their cause. These include the diseases caused by the staphylococcus bacteria – pneumonia is one such disease.

- **Diseases can be** either contagious (passed on by contact) or non-contagious.

- **Contagious diseases** are caused by germs such as bacteria and viruses (see germs). They include the common cold, polio, flu and measles. Their spread can be controlled by good sanitation and hygiene, and also by vaccination programmes.

▲ *This is a microscope photograph of a cancer cell.*

- **Non-contagious diseases** may be inherited or they may be caused by such things as eating harmful substances, poor nutrition or hygiene, getting old or being injured.

- **Endemic diseases** are diseases that occur in a particular area of the world, such as sleeping sickness in Africa.

- **Cancer** is a disease in which malignant cells multiply abnormally, creating growths called tumours.

- **Cancer kills** 6 million people a year around the world. The risk increases as you get older.

Germs

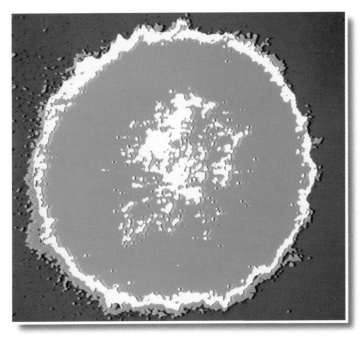

◀ *The disease AIDS (Acquired Immune Deficiency Syndrome) is caused by a virus called HIV (Human Immunodeficiency Virus). This virus gets inside vital cells of the body's immune system and weakens its ability to fight against other infections.*

- **Germs** are microscopic organisms that enter your body and cause harm.

- **The scientific word** for germ is 'pathogen'.

- **When germs** begin to multiply inside your body, you are suffering from an infectious disease.

- **An infection** that spreads throughout your body (flu or measles, for example) is called a systemic infection.

- **An infection** that affects only a small area (such as dirt in a cut) is called a localized infection.

- **It is often the reaction** of your body's immune system to the germ that makes you feel ill.

- **Bacteria** are single-celled organisms. They are found almost everywhere in huge numbers, and multiply rapidly.

- **Most bacteria are harmless,** but there are three harmful groups – cocci are round cells, spirilla are coil-shaped, and bacilli are rod-shaped. These harmful bacteria cause diseases such as tetanus and typhoid.

- **Viruses** can only live and multiply by taking over other cells – they cannot survive on their own. They cause diseases such as colds, flu, mumps and AIDS.

- **Parasites** are animals such as tapeworms that may live in or on your body, feeding on it and making you ill.

- **Fungal spores** and tiny organisms called protozoa can also cause illness.

▶ *When germs attack our immune system, our bodies react by fighting back strongly. This often makes us feel unwell.*

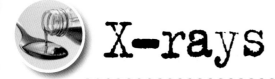

X-rays

▲ *Doctors have been using X-rays in their diagnosis since the end of the nineteenth century.*

- **X-rays** are a form of electromagnetic radiation, as are radio waves, microwaves, visible light and ultraviolet. They all travel as waves, but have different wavelengths.

- **X-ray waves** are much shorter and more energetic than visible light waves. X-rays are invisible because their waves are too short for our eyes to see.

- **X-rays are made** when negatively charged particles called electrons are fired at a heavy plate made of the metal tungsten. The plate bounces back X-rays.

● **Even though they are invisible** to our eyes, X-rays register on photographic film.

● **X-rays are so energetic** that they pass through some body tissues like a light through a net curtain.

● **To make an X-ray photograph,** X-rays are shone through the body. The X-rays pass through some tissues and turn the film black, but are blocked by others, leaving white shadows on the film.

● **Each kind of tissue** lets X-rays through differently. Bones are dense and contain calcium, so they block X-rays and show up white on film. Skin, fat, muscle and blood let X-rays through and show up black on film.

● **X-ray radiation** is dangerous in high doses, so the beam is encased in lead, and the radiographer who takes the X-ray picture stands behind a screen.

● **X-rays are** very good at showing up bone defects. So if you break a bone, it will probably be X-rayed.

● **X-rays also** reveal chest and heart problems.

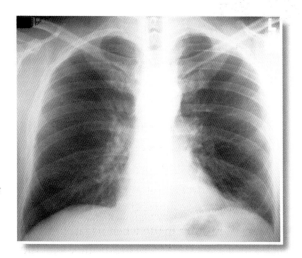

▶ *An X-ray gives a clear picture of the inside of the chest, showing the ribs, the spine and the branching airways in the lung. Any lung problems and blockages show up as white shadows.*

Scans

▲ *MRI scans are particularly valuable for providing clear images of the brain and spinal cord.*

- **Diagnostic imaging** means using all kinds of complex machinery to make pictures or images of the body to help diagnose and understand a problem.

- **Many imaging techniques** are called scans, because they involve scanning a beam around the patient, to and fro in lines or waves.

- **CT scans** rotate an X-ray beam around the patient while moving him or her slowly forward. This gives a set of pictures showing different slices of the patient's body.

- **CAT** stands for computerized axial tomography.

- **MRI scans** surround the patient with such a strong magnet that all the body's protons (tiny atomic particles) turn the same way. A radio pulse is then used to knock the protons in and out of line, sending out radio signals that the scanner picks up to give the picture.

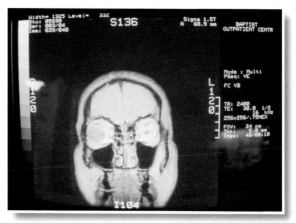

▲ *One of a series of CAT scans of the head and brain.*

- **MRI** stands for magnetic resonance imaging.

- **PET scans** involve injecting the patient with a mildly radioactive substance, which flows around with the blood and can be detected because it emits (gives out) particles called positrons.

- **PET** stands for positron emission tomography.

- **PET scans** are good for seeing how blood flow alters to a particular part of the body.

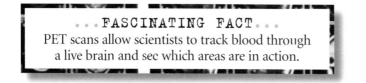

···FASCINATING FACT···
PET scans allow scientists to track blood through
a live brain and see which areas are in action.

Operations

- **A surgical operation** is when a doctor cuts or opens up a patient's body to repair or remove a diseased or injured body part.

- **An anaesthetic** is a drug or gas that either sends a patient completely to sleep (a general anaesthetic), or numbs part of the body (a local anaesthetic).

- **Minor operations** are usually done with just a local anaesthetic.

- **Major operations** such as transplants are done under a general anaesthetic.

- **Major surgery** is performed by a team of people in a specially equipped room called an operating theatre.

- **The surgical team** is headed by the surgeon. There is also an anaesthetist to make sure the patient stays asleep, as well as surgical assistants and nurses.

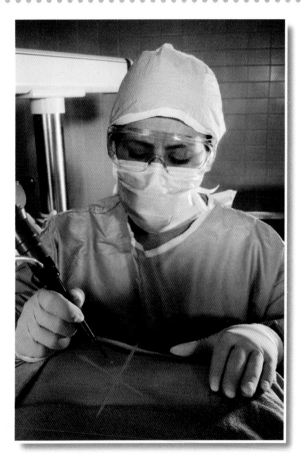

▲ In some operations, laser beams are used instead of the standard surgical knife, as they allow more control and precision, and reduce the risk of damage or bleeding.

198

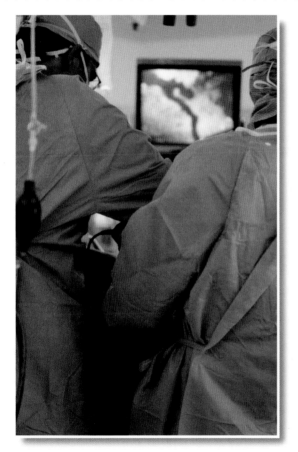

▲ *Many tricky operations are now performed using miniature cameras which help the surgeon see tiny details inside the body.*

- **The operating theatre** must be kept very clean to prevent an infection entering the patient's body during the operation.

- **In microsurgery,** a microscope is used to help the surgeon work on very small body parts such as nerves or blood vessels.

- **In laser surgery**, the surgeon cuts with a laser beam instead of a scalpel, and the laser seals blood vessels as it cuts. It is used for delicate operations such as eye surgery.

- **An endoscope is** a tube-like instrument with a TV camera at one end. It can be inserted into the patient's body during an operation to allow surgeons to look more closely at body parts.

Drugs

- **Antibiotic drugs** are used to treat bacterial infections such as tuberculosis (TB) or tetanus. They were once grown as moulds (fungi) but are now made artificially.

- **Penicillin** was the first antibiotic drug, discovered in a mould in 1928 by Alexander Fleming (1881–1955).

- **Analgesic drugs** such as aspirin relieve pain, working mainly by stopping the body making prostaglandin, the chemical that sends pain signals to the brain.

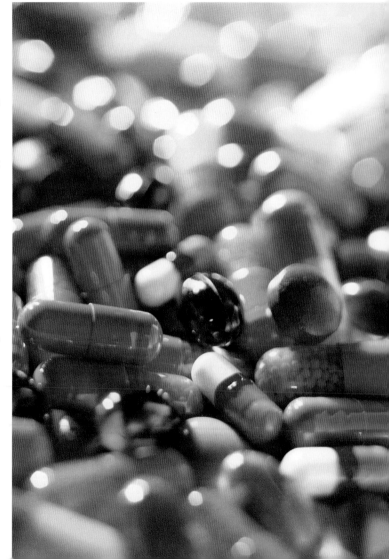

▶ *Thousands of different drugs are today used to treat illness.*

- **Tranquillizers** are drugs that calm. Minor tranquillizers are drugs such as prozac, used to relieve anxiety.

- **Major tranquillizers** are used to treat mental illnesses such as schizophrenia.

- **Psychoactive drugs** are drugs that change your mood. Many, including heroin, are dangerous and illegal.

- **Stimulants** are drugs that boost the release of the nerve transmitter noradrenaline, making you more lively and awake. They include the caffeine in coffee.

- **Narcotics,** such as morphine, are powerful painkillers that mimic the body's own natural painkiller, endorphin.

- **Depressants** are drugs such as alcohol which do not depress you, but instead slow down the nervous system.

▲ *Alexander Fleming was a British bacteriologist. His discovery in 1928 of the life-saving antibiotic, penicillin, opened a new era for medicine.*

. . . FASCINATING FACT . . .
In future, more drugs may be made by microbes or animals with altered genes. Insulin is already made in the pancreas of pigs.

Transplants

- **More and more body parts** can now be
  replaced, either by transplants (parts taken
  from other people or animals) or by implants
  (artificial parts).

- **Common transplants** include: the kidney, the
  cornea of the eye, the heart, the lung, the liver
  and the pancreas.

- **Some transplant organs** (such as the heart,
  lungs and liver) are taken from someone who
  has died.

- **Other transplants** (such as the kidney) may be
  taken from living donors.

- **After the transplant organ** is taken from the
  donor, it is washed in an oxygenated liquid and
  cooled to preserve it.

- **One problem** with transplants is that the body's
  immune system identifies the transplant as
  foreign and attacks it. This is called rejection.

▶ *These are just some of the artificial implants now put
in place – hip, knee, shoulder and elbow. Old people often
need implants to replace joints that have deteriorated.*

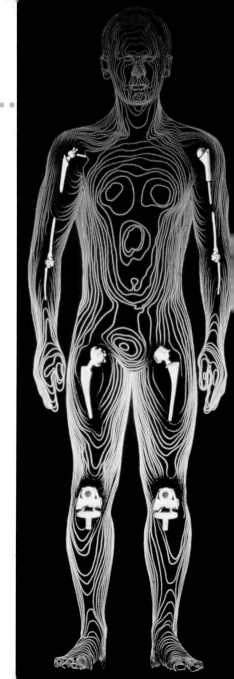

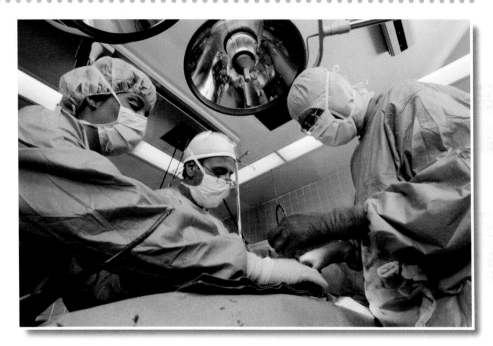

▲ *Most organ transplant operations last several hours. The patient must then remain in hospital for up to four weeks, depending on the particular organ that has been transplanted.*

● **To cut down** the chance of rejection, patients may be given drugs such as cyclosporin to suppress their immune system.

● **Heart transplant** operations last 4 hours.

● **During a heart transplant**, the patient is connected to a heart-lung machine which takes over the heart's normal functions.

Fitness

- **Fitness** is about how much and what kind of physical activity you can do without getting tired or strained.

- **Fitness depends** on your strength, flexibility (bendiness) and endurance (staying power).

- **One key to fitness** is cardiovascular fitness – that is, how well your heart and lungs respond to the extra demands of exercise.

- **One measure of cardiovascular fitness** is how quickly your pulse rate returns to normal after exercise – the fitter you are, the quicker it returns.

- **Another measure of cardiovascular fitness** is how slowly your heart beats during exercise – the fitter you are, the slower it beats.

◀ *Skiing is one of the most demanding of all sports, and top skiers need to be extremely fit to cope with the extra strain on their bodies.*

- **Being fit** improves your physical performance.

- **Being fit** can often protect against illness.

- **Being fit** can slow down the effects of ageing.

- **Cardiovascular fitness** reduces the chances of getting heart disease.

- **Fitness tests** involve comparing such things as height, weight and body fat, and measuring blood pressure and pulse rate before and after exercise.

◀ *Many people keep fit by attending exercise classes.*

Exercise

- **When you exercise,** your muscles have to work much harder than normal, so need much more oxygen and glucose (a kind of sugar) from the blood.

- **To boost oxygen,** your heart beats twice as fast and pumps twice as much blood, and your lungs take in ten times more air with each breath.

- **To boost glucose,** adrenalin triggers your liver to release its store of glucose.

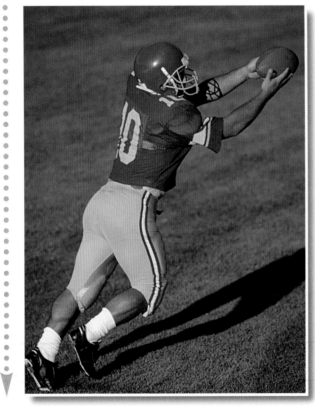

- **If oxygen delivery** to muscles lags, the muscles fill up with lactic acid, affecting your body for hours afterwards and sometimes causing painful cramp.

- **The fitter you are,** the quicker your body returns to normal after exercise.

- **Aerobic exercise** is exercise that is long and hard enough for the oxygen supply to the muscles to rise enough to match the rapid burning of glucose.

◀ *A sportsman such as a football player builds up his body's ability to supply oxygen to his muscles by regular aerobic training.*

...FASCINATING FACT...
When you exercise hard, your body burns
up energy 20 times as fast as normal.

▲ *Swimming is excellent for improving overall fitness, but without putting too much strain on the muscles and joints.*

● **Regular aerobic exercise** strengthens your heart and builds up your body's ability to supply extra oxygen through your lungs to your muscles.

● **Regular exercise** multiplies muscle fibres and strengthens tendons.

● **Regular exercise** can help reduce weight when it is combined with a controlled diet.

207

Index

Index

Index

Index

Index

Index

Index

Index

Acknowledgements

The publishers would like to thank the following artists who
have contributed to this book:

Peter Gregory, Rob Jakeway, Janos Marffy, Annabel Milne,
Tracy Morgan, Terry Riley, Mike Saunders, Rudi Vizi

The publishers would like to thank the following sources for
the use of their photographs:

Science Pictures Limited/CORBIS: Page 72

All other pictures from the Miles Kelly Archives.